The Healing Power of Forgiving

The Healing Power of Forgiving

Martha Alken, O.P.

A *Crossroad* Book
The Crossroad Publishing Company
New York

1997

The Crossroad Publishing Company
370 Lexington Avenue, New York, NY 10017

All scripture used in this book is taken from *The Catholic Study Bible: New American Bible* (New York: Oxford University Press, 1990).

Printed in the United States of America

Library of Congress Cataloguing-in-Publication Data

Alken, Martha.
The healing power of forgiving / Martha Alken.
p. cm.
Includes bibliographical references.
ISBN 0-8245-1597-8 (pbk.)
1. Forgiveness—Religious aspects—Christianity. I. Title.
BV4647.F55A54 1997
234'.5—dc21

97-4154
CIP

To my family

and

To my Sinsinawa Dominican Sisters

who have been my support

and teachers of forgiving

Acknowledgments

My first debt of gratitude goes to the members of the communities I lived in while writing this book, especially my sisters: Joeann, Marci, Maureen, Doris, and Jeri. I am grateful for the encouragement, patience, and support they showered upon me. I thank my family and friends, who supported me in a myriad of ways with stories, humor, questions, insights, and faith in the creative process.

I am particularly grateful to Patricia Burke. Many of the themes found in the last chapter of this book have their foundation in her inspiring retreat direction. Upon this foundation, I was able to build a house of forgiving with the encouragement of Stella Storch, O.P., who advocated and supported my studies on forgiveness among faculty, staff, and parishioners of Blessed Sacrament Church in Madison, Wisconsin. I am grateful for the fine-tuning of the initial work on forgiveness by my advisor, Homer Ashbey. I wish to thank Lynn Schmitt Quinn, who is so pastoral that she makes editing a book truly a ministry.

Finally, I owe a special debt of gratitude to the persons who entrusted me with their stories. Though revealing pain, these stories also reflect the magnanimity of the human spirit. These stories restore faith in our capacity to love and forgive unconditionally.

Contents

The stories presented in this book are often a composite:
names have been changed and events altered
to assure confidentiality
while remaining true to the message.

1

The Human Need to Forgive

A Question of Power

It struck like a bolt of lightning! We had just completed a very good meeting with parents preparing their children to receive the sacrament of reconciliation. During our closing prayer, I had asked each person to read aloud and share his or her reflections on a scripture quotation about forgiveness. Insights were profound and the prayers inspirational. The pastor drew John 20:22–23: "Receive the Holy Spirit. Whose sins you forgive are forgiven them. And whose sins you retain are retained." I enthusiastically said, "Isn't it fitting that the one priest among us should receive the word we normally attribute to the power of the priest during the sacrament of reconciliation?" Suddenly, I realized that I felt angry and wondered why. Later I found myself questioning why this power to forgive is reserved for the ordained priest when experience shows us that each human person exercises it many times over. Besides the obvious special aspect of the nature of the sacrament, I wondered if there were any other differences between the forgiveness a priest confers and the forgiveness we extend to one another on a personal level.

One difference that came quickly to mind was that in person-to-person forgiveness it is the one who has suffered from the wrongdoing, the one who has been wounded, who must extend forgiveness. What gives people the magnanimity and compassion to transcend perfectly normal feelings of anger and hurt after some deep wound and forgive those who have hurt them? The dynamic of forgiveness for the ordinary person requires a sacrifice on the part of the one who forgives that a priest does not have to make in offering forgiveness during the sacrament of reconciliation.

The idea for a book about our own power to heal through forgiving was conceived that night.

In the Catholic tradition the words from John 20 quoted above are attributed specifically to the priestly power of absolving sins in confession. The priest absolves in the name of God and as an official representative of the church. Catholic Christians can hardly discuss the power to forgive without reference to the sacrament of reconciliation. We Catholics need to reclaim our power to forgive, which is then celebrated in the sacrament.[1]

What gives a person the courage and greatness of soul that are needed to forgive? We have all seen people who have had similar injurious experiences; some are left embittered, self-pitying and small of heart, others develop a Buddha-like half smile as a permanent feature, and still others are moved to serving their neighbors. Wherein lies the difference?

There are two vital ingredients: the spiritual depth with which one has lived life, and proficiency in the art of letting go. Compassionate persons have learned the lessons of forgiving. They realize that holding on to injury hurts them doubly. Offering forgiveness brings healing to oneself and to the human community.

We see many "walking wounded" in our day. Their obvious pain compels us to look at the healing power that forgiving may bring to their lives. Serious injuries that leave us with open wounds include the death of a parent, loss of a child, betrayal by a friend, marital infidelity, abuse, addiction, neglect, rejection, incest, theft, false accusation, and systemic oppression. Untended, such injuries lead to physical illness, psychological distress, spiritual malaise, and social violence. If we do not forgive, we relive the pain over and over again. Serious injury compounded by unreleased resentment creates a third wound, its own physical and psychological suffering. Why, then, is it so difficult to forgive?

It is difficult, first, because misconceptions about forgiving abound. Forgiveness is seen by some as weakness, as remaining the victim, or as spiritual one-upmanship. No wonder they shy away from it! Second, some people hang on to the benefit derived from being wounded. They identify themselves with the pain. Third, still others suppress the hurt and deny the injury until a crisis forces them to face the original wound and the question of forgiving. Holding on to an injury hurts the person twice over; there is the original wound, and there are the damaging effects of harboring resentment. Forgiveness brings healing to both. Forgiveness alleviates distress and anxiety, it restores the ability to relate, and it enhances social harmony. Forgiving is the choice that opens us to a gift of grace. A major focus of this book is around the question: How do the need to forgive, the power to choose, and the movement of grace interact in the process of forgiving? This question is explored from the perspective of one who has been wronged and makes a decision to forgive, despite a legitimate right to resentment. "If we are to forgive," Joanna North writes, "our resentment is to be overcome not by denying ourselves the right to that resentment, but by endeavoring to view the wrongdoer with compassion, benevolence and love while recognizing that he has willfully abandoned his right to them."[2] *Forgiving* is a verb, an action word. It is a choice we make. Forgiving is a life-stance, a mode of being, by which we further the life of God among us.

The question of power arises when we explore the desire to forgive. Forgiving gives us power in that we become an instrument for healing. We do not forgive from a *position of power*, however, for that is mercy or legal pardon. Doris Donnelly states, "Forgiveness is a power . . . a directing force in my life, an energizing influence. . . . Forgiveness is a power that says that as deep as the pain may be, there is a strength and a comfort in the pain so that I am finally led not by the wound but by a force more commanding than the hurt."[3] Power, in and of itself, is neutral. We use it positively or abuse it negatively. It is a human trait and, as such, has its own integrity. Arendt writes, "Power is actualized only where word and deed have not parted company, where words are not empty and deeds not brutal, where words are not used to veil intentions but to disclose realities, and deeds are not used to violate and destroy but to establish relations and create new realities."[4] Personal power is essential to Jesus' message of forgiveness. God, as well as the human person, exerts the power to forgive. As a matter of fact, God's act of forgiving may be contingent upon our own. "When you stand to pray, forgive anyone against whom you have a grievance so that your heavenly Father may in turn forgive you your transgressions" (Mk 11:25). In other words, "Stop judging, that you may not be judged. For as you judge, so will you be judged, and the measure with which you measure will be measured out to you" (Mt 7:1-2).

A Philosophical Perspective

Philosophers—lovers of wisdom—have expounded on the nature of forgiveness for centuries. The Christian tradition offers a unique perspective on forgiveness. Its contribution is recognized in the secular realm, as well. Hannah Arendt reminds us that "the discoverer of the role of forgiveness in the realm of human affairs was Jesus of Nazareth."[5] Virgil Elizondo agrees: "Jesus broke the cycle of offense for offense. In this he initiated radical new possibilities for the human person, for human relations and for society at large."[6] Forgiving is a choice, an act of will, a human power, and a gift of grace. Arendt maintains that the power to forgive, as shown in Matthew 18:35 (cf. Mark 11:25; Matthew 6:14-15), is "primarily human power: God forgives 'us our debts, as we forgive our debtors.'"[7] God forgives us in the same measure as we forgive. Forgiving is necessary for human growth and development. Not forgiving keeps us stuck, dull, trapped, and relationally stagnant. Arendt continues, "Without being forgiven, released from the consequences of what we have done, our capacity to act would, as it were, be confined to one single deed from which we could never recover; we would remain the victims of its consequences forever."[8] And Joanna North concludes, "Forgiveness [is] the natural completion of a process of restoring and healing the relation which the wrongdoer has, for a time, suspended."[9]

Forgiving restores our hope in the future. The relationship may not be reconciled, but once we forgive, the relationship is no longer determined by the pain of the past. Forgiven relationships are open to the future. Forgiving releases resentment and restores harmony of heart.

Philosophers Hannah Arendt and Joanna North and theologian Doris Donnelly take an active approach toward power. Could it be that the emphasis on human power as positive and necessary comes from a feminist perspective? Certainly women have had to exert their power in a variety of ways, just to survive. And is the notion of God's "initiating" a masculine paradigm? George Soares-Prabhu writes, "All forgiveness, like all love, of which forgiveness is a particular form, originates from God, who has loved and forgiven us first (I Jn. 4:7, 21; Lk. 7:47; Mt. 18:23-35)."[10] Elizondo says forgiveness is always offered by God. We choose to share in that power—or not. "In forgiving others, I ratify and make my very own God's generous offer of universal forgiveness. . . . Thus it is in forgiving that I am divinised: to err is human, to forgive divine!"[11]

Proponents of forgiveness agree that forgiving happens from a position of strength. Forgiveness is not a method of hiding our shame or protecting our fragile inner self. Forgiving is a process that is idiosyncratic. It is colored by strength of character, family history, social environment, and culture. Consequences of not forgiving lead to self-preoccupation, anger, isolation, high blood pressure, and other negative ways of being. Those who do not forgive are angry people, directed by negative memories. They live with little self-worth, and their relationships are strained.[12] Forgiving, on the other hand, offers injured persons freedom from the burden of resentment. It may assuage some of the guilt of wrongdoers, even though we can all "expect to suffer the lingering tremors of residual guilt."[13]

A PSYCHOLOGICAL IMPERATIVE

Forgiving—releasing another or oneself from rightful resentment—is an imperative, a necessity for healing the psyche. For the past decade Robert Enright, a professor in the educational psychology department at the University of Wisconsin, has conducted cross-cultural studies on the topic of forgiveness. He presents the following philosophical and psychological refinements as a framework for his research:

- Forgiveness occurs between people.
- Forgiveness occurs after serious injustice and deep hurt.
- Understanding of injustice precedes forgiveness.
- The forgiveness journey may take time.
- Forgiveness can be lovingly unconditional, requiring nothing of the other.
- Forgiveness can be transforming of self, the other, and the community.[14]

Forgiving Another

Though forgiving addresses an injurer and an inflicted wound, it is a private act that has very public consequences. It takes a strong sense of self and much courage to forgive serious wrong. Forgiving, the foreswearing of judgment in the face of serious injury, calls forth compassion and magnanimity of soul. Forgiveness is light years away from indifference.

Forgiveness presumes an understanding of justice. Forgiveness is directed toward wrongdoing that is intentional and carries with it a moral responsibility. It is not to be confused with condoning, mercy, pardon, or justification. We may forgive, but we cannot control the legal consequences the wrongdoer has incurred. Justice remains. True forgiveness does not deny the depth of our pain. Nor is forgiving a method of self-help. It is not motivated by one-upmanship. There is no co-dependency in real forgiveness. Forgiving does not mean we accept responsibility for the offense, which is not ours. Self-denigrating statements such as, "If only . . . " and "If I hadn't . . . " reflect a victim mentality. Forgiving calls forth a change in our self-definition. It moves us from being the "victim" to being the "agent" of our life's situation. When talking with my friend Joan about this point of the book, she said simply, "The act of forgiveness is the act of agency." Forgiving is not forgetting the injury. Rather, when we forgive, we let go of the power our minds have to entrap us by replaying old tapes and rekindling fires of pain and resentment with each memory. Erasing those negative mental tapes is the only kind of "forgetting" that cauterizes wounds and allows for the possibility of healing. Forgiveness is not yet reconciliation. Forgiving frees the heart; reconciliation reunites it with the offender's. They are separate but related movements of grace, God's life, in us.

As Unconditional Regard

Joanna North stresses that unconditional forgiveness is ultimately a choice: "Forgiveness is a matter of a willed change of heart—the successful result of an active endeavor to replace bad thoughts with good, bitterness and anger with compassion and affection. . . . Simply ceasing to be angry . . . cannot be called forgiveness. Forgiveness requires no repentance, amends, regret or retribution [from the offender] . . . though these may be helpful."[15] Forgiving is not conditional on whether the wrongdoer asks for forgiveness, expresses sorrow, makes amends, or engages in any other reconciliatory behavior. True forgiveness is "offered unconditionally. . . . [It] draws the other in love and benefits the one wronged, the wrongdoer, the relationship and perhaps even the community."[16] It is through such unconditionality that we image our God. Non-foreclosure and spontaneity are hallmarks of a forgiving heart. The past no longer determines the future. We have not shut down; the future has potential. We come to see that loving and forgiving without self-interest are possible and healthy. They are our call to greatness.

For Self-Preservation

Beverly Flanigan addresses the question of forgiving the unforgivable. She defines *unforgivable* as betrayal by intimate injurers, moral wounds that assault a person's most fundamental belief system.[17] What is unforgivable about injuries is the breaking of trust, the shattering of our belief systems. The particular wound and the residue, the aftermath, need forgiving. Flanigan claims the core of forgiveness is a conversion of mind. We think differently about ourselves, the injurer, and the wounding, but we do so out of self-preservation. I propose that forgiving does heal the self, but it is more than self-healing or self-help. John Hebl and Robert Enright strongly maintain that unconditional love, not psychological well-being, is the core of forgiveness. "One who forgives has suffered a deep hurt, usually revealing an underlying resentment; the offended person has a moral right to resentment, but overcomes it nonetheless; a new response to the other accrues, including compassion and love; this loving response occurs despite the realization that there is no *obligation* to love the offender."[18] Healing occurs as a byproduct of magnanimity, compassion, and courage that precede and follow upon the choice to forgive.

Flanigan says the process for forgiving entails claiming the injury, blaming the injurer, balancing the scales, and choosing to forgive. Simon and Simon also present a concrete process for recovering from the damage of serious personal injury. According to them, there are six stages in forgiving: denial, self-blame, victim, indignation, survivor, and integration.[19] They claim we start, stop, and move again and again through the process. Naming and acknowledging the wrong as injustice is a primary step in the healing process of forgiving. This in itself takes courage; forgiving is engaged in from a position of strength and is ultimately a matter of choice. Knowledge of the injury and the desire to forgive are prerequisites for that moment of grace when healing and forgiving happen. In forgiving, injured and injurer alike are set free and offered renewed hope, a new future. As Joan Borysenko writes, "Old hurts cannot be cancelled and undone, but these emotions can become the seeds of transcendence that allow healing to occur whether we are the victim or the aggressor."[20]

Something Discovered

John Patton approaches forgiveness from a pastoral-care perspective. He claims the core of forgiveness is the discovery that the injured person can commit the same evil as the wrongdoer: There, but for the grace of God, go I. The more one makes the choice to forgive, the more one realizes the need to be forgiven. "I am more like those who have hurt me than different from them."[21] In other words, Patton believes human forgiveness is a discovery rather than an attitude or an act. "Why, then," asks Enright, "does scripture and Jesus teach us in particular about forgiveness and not just leave it to be discovered?"[22] Giving and receiving forgiveness are forms of one-upmanship, according to

Patton. Forgiving gives the one who has been injured a sense of self-righteousness and moral superiority vis-à-vis the wrongdoer.

Flanigan also rejects the discovery approach by reminding us of the dangers of "mirroring the injury." In this early stage of the forgiving process, when we feel that we could, in like circumstances, commit the same wrong, there is a sense of equality. When the wounded wound, they balance the scale. They may become more empathetic and even reach out in compassion and forgiveness to the one who injured them. However, perpetrating a similar injury is self-destructive and forecloses on choices available to the injured. "No one wins; everyone loses. . . . If forgiveness flows from knowing oneself as a person capable of hurting others, forgiveness has come with a very high price tag."[23]

Forgiving may instill a sense of self-righteousness if we tell the wrongdoer that he or she has been forgiven. It is not essential to do so. Forgiving is inner work that bears fruit in altered behavior. True forgiveness helps us let go of the very idea of superiority. Borysenko points out: "As long as we continue to identify with one side of the coin exclusively—debtor or creditor—we remain psychologically one-up or one-down on the other person. Forgiveness requires us to give up our ideas of better or worse and to finally see ourselves as equals and co-learners."[24]

Patton's position that forgiveness occurs in the discovery of personal vulnerability and sinful culpability seems to be only part of the truth. There is choice, and there is grace. Realizing our capacity for wrongdoing no more assures forgiveness than saying that because we are aware of the psychological benefit of forgiving, we therefore forgive. Yet, there are stories that seem to corroborate Patton's discovery theory. One of these is the story of a man named Hank.

Hank held back the tears with great effort as he told his story. Years later, he was still devastated by his wife's infidelity. The betrayal had hurt deeply. He explained it as the classic textbook example of a mid-life crisis. His wife apologized and "did all the right things." He wanted to forgive, willed it, prayed for it. Hank read all kinds of books about forgiveness. It did not happen until last year. He fell in love with another woman and was, himself, tempted to be unfaithful. It was the awareness that he, too, could fall in love and want another, that enabled him to forgive his wife. He no longer has a "moral superiority" that asks, "How could you break a contract?" The wound is not forgotten, it is part of their history. But Hank now speaks out of compassion, as well as intellectual knowledge, when it comes to the question of forgiving.

It seems that Patton's discovery theory of forgiveness is one fragment of the prism of forgiving. He catches the moment of compassion, whereas Raymond Studzinski reflects the aspect that it is an integration of the pain of one's past with hope for the future. Studzinski says, "Forgiveness is an acceptance of what has happened as past and as not the final word on the other or on oneself. It is an act of integration in which the painful event is incorporated into one's personal history as a past event but one that does not foreclose the future."[25]

John's story also supports Patton's discovery theory.

John, at age twenty-three, wanted his father to be part of his life again. When John was eight years old, his father and mother went through a bitter divorce. His father, a truck driver, managed to sign up for routes that would bring him into town so he would be accessible to his children. But each visit meant crossing paths with his former wife. This presented the potential for renewed arguments and fights. His visits sparked such emotional trauma that after a while they became less frequent, then negligible. John felt abandoned and had a tumultuous, troubled adolescence.

Fifteen years after his parents' divorce, John's girlfriend announced that she no longer wanted to see him nor did she want him to contact their child. Another generation, another abandoned son. John now understood his father's plight. He now could forgive his own father and reclaim his love.

Forgiveness addresses an injured relationship—what was good has been damaged. Joseph Beatty says, "The precondition for forgiveness, then, is the existence of a positive relation which is disturbed . . . by the offense itself."[26] Betrayal and abandonment are offenses that "disturb" a relationship of trust. When we recognize ourselves as capable of that same "disturbance," we discover forgiveness. Perhaps this discovery is but a crack in the door that allows us a peek at possibilities for healing. Perhaps the discovery of our own need for forgiveness is but an invitation to choose to forgive, because we have seen that we share a common human nature.

✦ *Prayer Experience* ✦

When we choose to forgive another, we embark on a healing journey. The itinerary for our life's journey includes rest stops along the way. These stops include joy, pain, sorrow, remorse. But each of these are only "rest stops," and we are not to make them "home." After the call to prayer, a song such as "Healing Journey"[27] provides a good opening reflection with its message that all of us are on a healing journey, but we make that journey one by one and step by step.

Spend today reflecting on your life and the pain you wish to expel from your heart. As you walk outside, collect a stone or pebble to represent each injury that still lies heavy on your heart. Carry the stone(s) with you throughout the day.

In the evening, gather with loved ones or in a supportive community. Come together to pray around a well, real or symbolic. Replay the healing song you have chosen and recall that it is possible, though paradoxical, to love unconditionally. We can love without seeking a specific reward. True love is without self-interest. Is it also possible to forgive unconditionally, seeking nothing from the other. Listen to the following scriptures:

> If you, O LORD, mark iniquities,
> LORD, who can stand?
> But with you is forgiveness,
> that you may be revered.
> —Psalm 130:3–4

> So he got up and went back to his father. While he was still a long way off, his father caught sight of him, and was filled with compassion. He ran to his son, embraced him and kissed him. (Lk 15:20)

Reflect in silence upon the following: We love and forgive others unconditionally out of a strong sense of self. The fourteenth-century mystic Catherine of Siena compares the quest for self-knowledge to digging down through the soil of our "well." We find there the spring of living waters. "Catherine encourages us not to be afraid of going down this well, that is, not to run away from the part of ourselves which seems . . . frail, small and imperfect, but rather to stay with this 'soil' for it is a reminder of our creatureliness and of our need for God who is the running, bubbling source of life within us. At the bottom of our well, at the centre of our being, therefore, we rejoice in God who is All."[28]

Share insights about what it was like for you to carry your stone(s) around with you all day. Did they get heavy? Tiresome? Did you mark them with symbols or names of persons who wronged you? Did you replay your mental tapes of the injury over and over? Are you now ready to let go of your resentment? If so, cast your stone, your burden of resentment, into the well. If not, if you want to hang on to your pain, keep the pebble in your palm.

Allow the stones you have cast into the well to be embraced, healed, and transformed by God's living water. According to Catherine of Siena, "As long as we love others by drawing from this fountain, our capacity to love will grow rather than diminish; only when we take the vessel of our heart out of the fountain will it become empty."[29] Drink deeply from the living waters of God. Know that we also find the life of God in one another. Therefore, go to another person and ask that individual to pray with you. Share a tangible sign of renewed peace of mind and heart.

Forgiving Ourselves

Mary was a sister in her fifties. As she lay dying of cancer, many persons came to her asking for her forgiveness. Some were former superiors from the "old days" who had made Mary's life as a young sister very difficult. Mary hardly remembered specific wrongs and was saddened by how those who came to her were suffering. These persons were aware they had injured her. They were wounded by the wrongs they had inflicted on Mary, although at the time, all was done out of perceived duty. Now they needed Mary's forgiveness to be able to let go of their own guilt and to forgive themselves.

The Great Commandment

Usually we are more ready to forgive another than to forgive ourselves. Parents, like the father of the prodigal son, are full of compassion toward children who have done wrong. Why do we struggle so hard to forgive ourselves, even though we believe God forgives us unconditionally? Maybe it is because we have not learned how to love ourselves. Hebrew and Christian scriptures teach us:

> He said to him, "You shall love the Lord, your God with all your heart, with all your soul, and with all your mind. This is the greatest and the first commandment. The second is like it: You shall love your neighbor as yourself. The whole law and the prophets depend on these two commandments." (Mt 22:37-40)

These are the guiding principles for holiness. Most of us seem to have a good grasp of loving God and of the necessity to love our neighbor. However, in our tradition self-love has been seen at worst as sinful and at best as something to "grow out of." Self-love is seen as the antithesis of true love, generous giving, and forgiving. Forgiveness is rooted in unconditional love. How can we assume to forgive ourselves if we do not have a solid core of unconditional self-love?

Fear of Narcissism

There seems to be an intricate connection between the inability to forgive ourselves and a misperception of narcissism. In traditional psychoanalytic theory, self-love or narcissism has been looked upon as a "fixation" or "regression" from healthy love of others. Psychologist Heinz Kohut does religion and psychology a great service by positing two rightful and separate lines of human development. Each line of development contains unhealthy to healthy growth patterns. Kohut says that unhealthy, disordered, archaic narcissistic persons are "easily hurt and offended, they become quickly over-stimulated, and their fears and worries tend to spread and become boundless."[30] Self-forgiveness for such persons is foreign and unimaginable.

Kohut helps us clarify the meaning of true self-love and perceive it as more than just an unhealthy form of "healthy" object-love. The narcissistic person is characterized by particularly low self-esteem and the inability to cope with injuries and slights to his or her vulnerable and fluid (rather than stable) inner being. Persons on this path of human growth tend to be hypersensitive to failure, especially public faux pas. They ruminate endlessly over their mistakes or over what they did not do, often driving themselves and others crazy with their "if only" scenarios.

Persons on a narcissistic track have a difficult time forgiving injury done to them by others. They find it well nigh to impossible to forgive themselves for having done harm. Perfectionism, a byproduct of the narcissistic personality, is their cross. For the narcissistic person, a self that is capable of wrongdoing is unforgivable. The personalities of narcissistic perfectionists are marred by a sense of shame. "Shame is an inner sense of being completely diminished or insufficient as a person. . . . A pervasive sense of shame is the ongoing premise that one is fundamentally bad, inadequate, defective, unworthy, or not fully valid as a human being."[31] The logical conclusion is that those who feel this way at the core of their being will have great difficulty forgiving themselves. Shame experienced in the narcissistic perfectionist is the product of early emotional wounding. As Wilkie Au and

Noreen Cannon state: "Narcissistic perfectionists have a poorly defined and weakly differentiated self. Because they lack a stable inner core, their sense of who they are is fragile, forcing them to rely on others' attention and admiration for their self-esteem."[32]

The narcissistic person's development follows its unique path toward wholeness. His or her needs along the way are normal. The human need for our existence to be significant is in a sense narcissistic—and also perfectly legitimate. We need to be understood and appreciated. When our needs are not met, we feel hurt. When the desires of our basic passions are thwarted, we claim injury. The longing for love and respect is normal and human. Until we accept our human needs as legitimate, forgiving ourselves for failures and for even having needs will be a struggle. Until we see legitimate narcissistic needs as normal to human growth, we will not be able to love with our whole heart, mind, and soul. Acceptance of our strengths, weaknesses, gifts, and needs enables us to tap into that reservoir of creative energy that bubbles up through the harmony of well-integrated wants and needs. It is the healing of the vulnerable inner structure of the narcissistic person that enables him or her to love the self, as distinct from others, realistically and legitimately. We all need to be found lovable, to be understood, and to be comforted. Having these needs met is as essential to our well-being as the air we breathe. Once we accept our human needs as legitimate, we can let go of self-condemnation and our fear of self-love. We may even go so far as to forgive ourselves as readily as we forgive others.

The narcissistic person moves toward a more healthy, mature, forgiving narcissism when he or she no longer looks solely to outside resources and persons for guidance, approval, and support. When we are healthy, we see God as a loving presence with whom we are connected and in union, while retaining our own identity. As we grow in wholeness, or holiness, we learn to trust our intuition, become more centered, and utilize our own inner resources to benefit ourselves and others. We are more able to let go of unreasonable fear and anxiety. Signs that this transformation is taking place are a sense of humor, a certain freedom that allows forgiving to be part of our self definition, and a deep pervasive peace. When we can laugh in the face of our own foibles, it is a sign that our demands for perfection and grandiosity have diminished and we have accepted our gifts and limitations. As we grow in wisdom, we "share in the acknowledgment of the fact that . . . not all has been solved. These frailties are now familiar and they can be contemplated with tolerance and composure."[33] The limitations of the self, and even the hurt that we have inflicted on others, are seen from the perspective of wisdom and have the potential to be forgiven.

✦ *Prayer Experience* ✦

It takes a strong sense of self to forgive another. A deeper "I AM" consciousness provides that sense. Following is a scripture reflection and guided meditation that lead toward greater self-knowledge. Start by reflecting on the words of a song such as "How Could Anyone"[34] that reaffirms the fact that our beauty, our perfection, our existence, our very being, loving, and forgiving—is a miracle!

Consider these words of scripture: "Now Jesus and his disciples set out for the villages of Caesarea Philippi. Along the way he asked his disciples, 'Who do people say that I am?' . . . And he asked them, 'But who do you say that I am?' Peter said to him in reply, 'You are the Messiah'" (Mk 8:27, 29). "I AM" is the first part of God's name. "I am who am" (Ex 3:14) is the source of the proper name of God, Yahweh. Who do you say *you* are? List twenty "I AM" statements while meditation music plays softly in the background. After a period of silent reflection, you may wish to articulate some of these self-affirmations to others.

Then relax with the following guided meditation:

Sit and breathe deeply, relax. Be aware of your body. Is there tension anywhere? If so, be attentive to it, breathe through it, and let the tension go. Beginning with your toes, breathe warm, healing light through each part of your body. As you reach the top of your head, complete the first deep inhalation; exhale, allowing the light to flow from the top of your head over your entire body like a waterfall. Do this several times until your find yourself in a state of bliss and gratitude. However awesome and beautiful your body is, you are not your body. With the next breath, let it go.

Now, as you breathe, recall the events prior to, during, and after an injury you feel that you want to forgive. Breathe through each event. What emotions are sparked in you by recalling your pain? You have emotions. You feel pain, joy, abandonment, fear, love, and so on. Emotions tell you that you are alive. But you are not your emotions. Leave them, with the next breath, for now.

You are not alone. You came to this moment from a family. You carry the pain of previous generations; their unfinished business is yours to complete. You live in the warmth of being loved, and with the pain of lost love. Perhaps anxiety over loved ones who suffer lies heavy on your heart. Persons with whom you share your life are part of you. But you are not your relationships. Let them go and come home to your self.

You may have already chosen to forgive. You know the benefit for yourself and for others of forgiving. You understand the damage that is done by clinging to resentment and anger. You have free will. You are intelligent. But you are not your mind. You are not your will. Let them go and for a moment be without a why.

You may have hopes for the future, a healed future. You may have plans for a new life. Preparation and planning are part of you. You are not your plans. Do not think, plan, or worry. Instead, come home to your self and to the arms of a loving, providential God. Be in the presence of the Spirit, our God, the lover of life, the giver of wisdom.

Let go of your body, emotions, relationships, mind, dreams, and even your will. What remains? Only, "I am." The fact of your existence is synonymous with the name of God. It is at this depth, in this soul space, that you realize "I am" and experience little distinction between self and God. Having come in contact with the infinite in yourself, take time and several deep breaths to reclaim each fine-tuned instrument of body, emotions, relationships, dreams, mind, and will that God has given you to play your melody of life. You have a body, emotions, relationships, hopes, plans, a mind, and a will. You are more than each or all of these. You also have wounds. You are more than your wounds. It is meeting the "I am" of your soul that enables you to accept the gifts and the limitations of your body, mind, personality, and relationships. Out of the strength of that "I am," you, and all wounded ones, can forgive unconditionally.[35]

A Social Necessity

We have seen that it takes a courageous act of will and a compassionate heart to forgive those who have injured us. Forgiving and refusing to forgive have rippling effects on all our relationships. The results of failure to forgive are broad, deep, and long-term, as seen in this therapist's negative reaction toward his client:

> I realized that he bore a physical resemblance to a person from my youth toward whom I still harbored a resentment. That insight was not enough for me to be able to remove the projected negative energy. I also had to go back to heal the original resentment.[36]

For Human Survival

Forgiving cuts to the core. Its healing happens from the inside out. Forgiving leaps time and generational boundaries. Forgiving traverses psychic and spiritual lands, as well.

Corrie ten Boom was a watchmaker's daughter in Haarlem, Holland. She became a heroine in the anti-Nazi movement and was sent to a concentration camp for hiding Jews. ten Boom tells of having to forgive the man who betrayed her during the war before she could, literally, sleep in peace. She recalls:

> Flames of fire seemed to leap around that name in my heart. I thought of father's final hours. . . . And I knew that if Jan Vogel stood in front of me now I could kill him. . . . All of me ached with the violence of the feelings about the man who had done us so much harm. . . . I was as guilty as Jan Vogel. . . . Didn't he and I stand together before an all-seeing God convicted of the same sin of murder? For I had murdered him with my heart and with my tongue. "Lord Jesus," I whispered . . . "I forgive Jan Vogel as I pray that You will forgive me. I have done him great damage. Bless him now . . . and his family." That night for the first time since our betrayer had a name I slept deep and dreamlessly until the whistle summoned us to roll call.[37]

As victims of concentration camps and other horrors of war came to recover at their home in Bloemendaal, ten Boom realized that for all these people, no matter what their particular wound, "the key to healing turned out to be the same. Each had a hurt he had to forgive: the neighbor who had reported him, the brutal guard, the sadistic soldier."[38] Today we have our own betrayers, those who are cruel, violent, and sadistic. While continuing the struggle for justice, we nevertheless need to learn what Corrie ten Boom learned fifty years ago: how to forgive unconditionally, for our own healing and for the sake of the world.

When forgiving is a lesson well learned, it enhances life for the whole community. Forgiving or non-forgiving has social ramifications. Forgiving is essential in a society where survival is based upon interdependent relationships. Forgiving becomes optional only when we think we do not need one another. Lance Morrow reminds us, "The process of forgetting as a substitute for forgiving may occur most readily in societies with a high rate of change, of physical and social mobility."[39] Whether society is interdependent or markedly individualistic, forgiving plays a pivotal role.

Teachers of Forgiving

There are many teachers of forgiveness in this world. One is Pope John Paul II. In 1984, after an attempt was made on his life, the pope visited Agca, his would-be assassin, and forgave him. Agca remained in prison. Forgiving does not deny justice. But forgiving teaches the world a lesson of courage and magnanimity of soul. Transformation is the result of forgiving. As Morrow points out, "What he [the pope] intended to show was a fundamental relationship between peace and the hearts of men and women, the crucial relevance of the turnings of will and spirit."[40] We choose to forgive. It may not always happen as immediately for us as it did for John Paul II, but the choice to forgive opens us up to new possibility.

Civil rights leaders, proponents of nonviolence, and victims of the Holocaust demonstrate that forgiving happens even under dire circumstances. The story of Etty Hillesum is a case in point. Hillesum, considered a contemporary mystic, was a Jewish woman who lived in Holland and died in Auschwitz in November 1943 at the age of twenty-nine. Her diaries and letters were composed during the last two years of her life but were not discovered until the 1980s. Her writings show that transformation, forgiving, and spiritual deepening are possible despite oppression and suffering.

Hillesum lived life fully, experienced her God intimately, suffered with dignity, and related compassionately with her persecutors. Just before her death in the camp, Hillesum wrote, "Give your sorrow all the space and shelter in yourself that is its due, for if everyone bears grief honestly and courageously, the sorrow that now fills the world will abate."[41] Hillesum's spirit remained undaunted and her greatness of soul shone forth in some of her last words:

> The misery here is really terrible and yet, often during the evening, I walk along the barbed wire with a spring in my step. And from deep in my heart comes a basic force saying, life is glorious and magnificent. Yet, we still need to build a whole new world. Against every new outrage and every fresh horror, we present another bit of love and goodness that comes from our very depths. . . . If we should survive unhurt in body and in soul, above all in soul, without bitterness and without hatred, then we shall have a right to "speak our piece" after the war. Maybe I am an ambitious woman but I would like to have a little to say.[42]

Hillesum's ambitions are being fulfilled as more and more of her work and spirit become known. She takes free, human initiative in her conversation with God. "With every heart-beat, it becomes more clear to me that you, God, cannot help us but we must help you to defend until the very end, that dwelling place, that home you have in us."[43] Hillesum showed us with her life that forgiving is essential for our own well-being and that of the world. It is necessary, if God is to survive among us. If we make a choice for forgiveness,then, with the help of God's grace, the path we take will become a road to inner freedom and peace. It is our choice and power, through forgiving, to keep the image of God alive amid sin that wishes to negate and destroy God's reality.

Conclusion

We may think that it is only the heroes and heroines of great persecutions who know how to forgive. Although theirs may be the more public calling, we all have our own demons, our own persecutors, our own oppressive systems that need the healing and liberation forgiveness offers. Forgiving both claims and releases the injury and, in the process, heals and bestows harmony on more than the self. Donnelly tells us:

> There is, of course, tremendous value in forgiving even if the act is not accepted. There is great value to the forgiver, who is free from the bondage of a heavy and hardened heart; there is enormous value to the community because of the ripple effect of all of our actions on everyone else. And though it is hard . . . to perceive, there is benefit to those who stand in need of forgiveness, because we have placed no barrier in

the way in the event that they recognize and acknowledge the offense as theirs.[44]

Forgiving frees the injured. Because we are interconnected, forgiving benefits the injurers, whether they know it or not. Forgiving adds to the level of goodness in the universe. Resentment, rightful though it is, detracts from it. Forgiving is key to transforming oppressive social, cultural, and religious systems. It assures us of a future after interpersonal, social, or systemic injury.

2

Forgiving and the Question of God

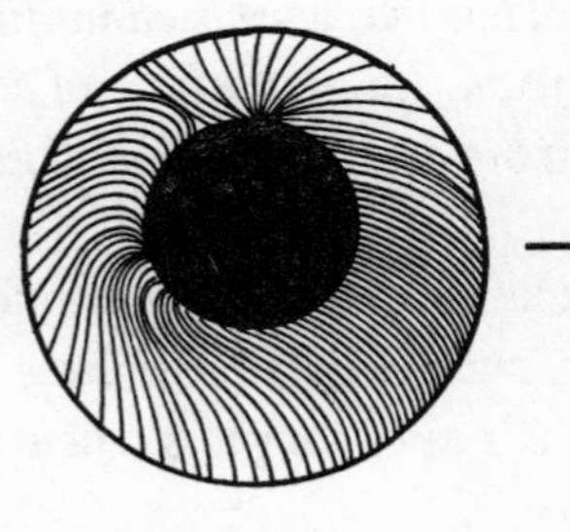

Introduction

Lost dreams rend the garment of our universe. Assumptions as to how the story of our life is to unfold are turned upside-down. Following are three examples of a future forever changed.

Broken Dreams

Jack's face looked old beyond his years. His hopes for a future in dairy farming were dashed to the ground. Gone was his dream "How can I forgive that guy?" he asked. The previous year Jack had bought ten cows at one thousand dollars each—his investment in a small dairy farm. The cows were impregnated too soon, and as a result, all died giving birth. Despite back-breaking labor, Jack had been unable to recover from the loss. He believed that the farmer who sold him the cows had cheated him out of his money, out of the family's financial security, and ultimately, out of his dream of becoming a successful dairy farmer. The guiding force of his life was now no longer a dream, but survival. Jack felt this had been the first of many setbacks. His farm goes up for auction this year. How can he forgive the theft of his dream? Asking the question is the first step. Putting it into the perspective of multiple causes is another.

A sister leaving a religious community takes with her not only the fruits of her education, which has been provided by the community, but her gifts and talents that have been nurtured in community. She takes with her a dream. Lost is the hope of a common future. A shared vision is left broken in the laps of those who remain.

The loss of a lover who marries someone else initiates feelings of anguish, anger, and betrayal. Lost is the dream of a life together. What needs to be sought is a new self-identification.

In each of these cases the hope for a certain future is banished. The pain of lost dreams is excruciating and the question of forgiveness eventually surfaces. Broken dreams are the fodder for forgiving.

A stolen dream, you say? *What if the thief in the night is God?* What if the structure of your universe is torn asunder and the assailant is God? What if your relationship to God is put to the question? Do you forgive? If you are a good person, like Job or the farmer who felt cheated out of his dream; if you are a reluctant prophet, like Jeremiah or the sister who remains holding a vision of community; if you are a lover, like Jesus or the woman who was abandoned for another, you know that the question of forgiving God is integral to journeying through the dark night of the soul.

Forgiving, if it is to be more than self-help, is rooted in our relationship to God. And this relationship is intimately connected to our image of God. The stories of Job and Jeremiah turn cultural and religious expectations of God inside out. God is transformed because of their lives; they are transformed in the process of coming to know that they do not know God. Their words and their lives teach us that "whoever seeks God in a definite mode accepts the mode and misses God, who is hidden in that mode."[1] It is through forgiving God for not being made in *our* image that we are freed and become transformed into God's image. Forgiving is the mystical experience of letting go, of losing and finding anew. When this experience takes us to God's doorstep, we come to the deepest questions of identity, meaning, and the purpose of human life—which is, simply, God.

THE PREDICAMENT OF JOB

Central to Job's predicament is the God question. Job is a good man who suffers loss, grief, and physical illness. Job's difficulties bring him to question why innocent people suffer, to attempt to identify the place of suffering in human life, to make some sense of it. Because of the predicament of Job, we wonder about the nature of God as just, as good, and as almighty. The people of Job's day saw God as the author of retributive justice, which rewards good and punishes evil. They presented an anthropocentric view of God—a perspective that is centered in the human person. God reacts to human beings, and therefore we determine our fate. Expectations that we call the shots concerning how God is to be for us are present with us yet. What if God does not meet our expectations? What if God seems to be lacking in power or in justice? What if our image of God is destroyed, our beliefs shattered, our paradigms turned inside out? Can we forgive? Whom do we need to forgive? Job's wife had a solution: "Are you still holding to your innocence? Curse God and die" (Jb 2:9). It took Job and his friends many more chapters to figure out the issue she stated so clearly. "Both in the original Hebrew book of Job and in many of the retellings of the story, Job's wife is the prototypical woman on the margin, whose iconoclastic words provoke defensive condemnation but whose insight serves as an irritant that undermines old complacencies."[2] The predicament for Job is the conflict between the reality of innocent suffering and the ideal of a good God. Job could not rely on the concepts of God presented by his friends. They matched his own and were proven inadequate. Job's friends preached to him, injecting their own notions of right and wrong, good and evil, and how God relates to both. Job had to suffer intensely, experience dishonor, be questioned and accused, and reframe his situation in order to see anew. Only then could he see that God was always with him, listening to his cries and his lament. "Job epitomizes the human longing for something more—a radically new awareness of God, of self, of world. . . . [Job] vigorously defended his integrity against his counselors' efforts to prove how sick and perverse he had become. And the integrity he defended was that of the *new* Job—victimized, dehumanized, and radicalized—emerging from the ashes of the status quo."[3]

Both Job and God were transformed as their relationship changed. God is beyond everything we can imagine. God is each label, and more than each label, we designate. God is greater than our expectations. That is a difficult lesson for us to learn. It is the conclusion Job eventually reached. It is the resolution of a mystic. Experiencing God as greater than our imaginings makes God beyond articulation.

Then Job answered the LORD and said:
I know that you can do all things,
and that no purpose of yours can be hindered.
I have dealt with great things that I do not understand;
things too wonderful for me, which I cannot know.
I have heard of you by word of mouth,
but now my eye has seen you.
Therefore, I disown what I have said,
and repent in dust and ashes.

—Job 42:1–6

Retributive Justice

A man suffering great pain during traumatic hospitalization weeps aloud, "Have I been so bad? Do I deserve this?" A woman cries out in frustration, "You owe me. I've been good!" Are these cries to God not two sides of the same coin of retributive justice? They reflect a theology that says good is rewarded and evil is punished. This was the predicament of Job. He held fast to the truth of his innocence, and still he suffered. He was not being rewarded for being good. How was he to deal with this breach of justice by the very Author of Justice?

You Owe Me!

The prevalent thinking in our culture is that if we work hard enough, we will get what we want. If we exercise and eat a balanced diet, we will be healthy. If we study, we will be successful. If we engage in fulfilling relationships, we will be happy. What if we do these things and still get sick? What if we get passed over for promotion or our relationship goes sour? Then, no doubt, we will wail "You owe Me! I've done all the right things." The following story is a contemporary example of Job's retributive justice predicament ("Elizabeth" is a composite of several sisters in mid-life).

Elizabeth's Story

Some years ago my path crossed Elizabeth's. We all need to be admired. Elizabeth, however, was the loud, gregarious life of the party who told stories with herself as their center. Relationships were like the spokes of a wheel with herself at the hub.

All of us deal with anxiety and worry, but for Elizabeth they were limitless. Life was one crisis after another. Her concerns filled the house, and the atmosphere around her was one of dramatic highs or lows. Soap operas paled in comparison. Elizabeth engaged in constant ruminations over her affairs. She experienced sleep disturbance during the night, and the anxious moments inevitable in day-to-day life turned into an all-pervading state of anxiety.

We all want to be taken seriously and have our feelings taken into account. Elizabeth, however, was hypersensitive to questions, criticism, or alternate proposals. She perceived these as rejections not only of her ideas but of her.

We need to identify with people or groups that share similar ideals. Certain people or experiences energize us all, but Elizabeth was overstimulated by the latest theology, charismatic leader, or health fad. Each provided a temporary sense of connectedness and became the source of her self-identity. As a result, her ministry was in a constant state of flux. Each new work was her life's calling.

It is normal and human to want to be with those we love. We seek the presence of those we admire and people who can comfort us in our need. Elizabeth went a little further. She followed persons in authority, claimed their friendship, and sought glory from their status. She was radiant when they looked with favor upon her. If someone in authority crossed her, disappointed or betrayed her, however, she would lash out against that person with a vehemence and intensity that matched her previous admiration. Apparently Elizabeth was attempting to get hold of her fragile, fluid self by constantly trying to declare who she was and that she mattered.

One day Elizabeth approached her community leader with what seemed an unreasonable and extravagant request for time, money, and support. To the leader's look of surprise, she responded, "You owe me. I've been good for over thirty years!"

This sense of entitlement is an attempt to hold together a fragile self. Elizabeth was protecting herself against disappointment and a great fear of trying to make it on her own. She presumed she had earned support by "being good." The irony is that she had a perfect right to support just for being herself. But it was this very sense of self that was lacking and that reduced her to bargaining, whining, and threatening.

Could this example of an unhealthy narcissistic personality be enlarged to identify a culture? The people during the time of Job? The people of today?

Grieving and Forgiving

When God does not act as God "should," when God disappoints us, then we, like Job and Jeremiah, have to ask if we can forgive God.

Forgive God? For some, this question is unthinkable. God is almighty. It is we who ask forgiveness of God. Others blame God as the cause of their grief. Rage against God is the predominant feeling for people like Andrew, whose wife had just had her second miscarriage in a year. For persons who have suffered great loss, forgiving God becomes the ultimate question.

To grieving families, whose whole being cries out "Why me?" Harold Kushner responds, "God does not reach down to interrupt the workings of laws of nature to protect the righteous from harm."[4] Kushner turned to scripture for solace after the untimely death of his son. He sought an answer to the question of why good people have to suffer, because he found the conventional answers to be less than satisfactory. In his reading of the Book of Job, Kushner saw three aspects that need to be weighed in the contemplation of suffering. One is that God is all-powerful; the second, that God is good and just; and the third, that Job is a good man.

All three beliefs can be maintained simultaneously if life is just fine. In the face of suffering, however, only two can be accepted. The question is, Which two? Job's friends accepted the first and second, that God is all-powerful, good, and just—therefore Job must have done something wrong. This is an example of a blaming the victim. Job upheld his own innocence and said that God is so powerful he does not need to be just.

The third alternative is presented by Kushner. Maybe God is not all-powerful. God has given us free will and abides by our choices and their consequences. Thus nature and human freedom, not God, are the causes of suffering. God intervenes by giving human beings the ability to transcend their pain and work together to reduce undeserved suffering. According to Kushner, God is not an innocent bystander; rather, God acts through us and speaks in us. Human beings are God's language. God answers our cry by coming to us in the incarnation of caring people. The ultimate question is not why we suffer, but how we respond in the face of suffering. Kushner concluded his reflection by asking some poignant questions:

> Are you capable of forgiving and accepting in love a world which has disappointed you by not being perfect . . . ? Are you capable of forgiving and loving the people around you, even if they have hurt you . . . ? Are you capable of forgiving and loving God even when you have found out that He

> is not perfect, even when He has let you down and disappointed you by permitting bad luck and sickness and cruelty in His world, and permitting some of those things to happen to you?[5]

We can answer yes to those questions only if our image of God includes compassion as well as incomprehensibility, immanence and nearness as well as transcendence and distance, nurturing as well as power, and forgiveness as well as justice. To answer yes to Rabbi Kushner's questions, we have to believe in a God who is not only the mystery of life, death, and resurrection but also of incarnation; a God who is with us in our suffering; a God who is willing to change and risk becoming what God was not—human. As Carl Jung says, "One should make clear to oneself what it means when God becomes man. It means nothing less than a world-shaking transformation of God."[6] In this awesome realization, we pray: Teach us your ways, O God, those ways of compassionate loving, your ways of unconditional forgiving, and give us the means of entering into earth-shaking transformations.

The Case of Jeremiah

Jeremiah struggled with a disappointing God. "We know from his own words that he was a quiet, peace-loving mystic sent by God, against his inclinations, to rebuke kings, accuse his fellow Jews of infidelity to the covenant, and draw upon himself in return the scorn, contempt, and homicidal hatred of his enemies."[7] During all this, he counted on God for support but felt that God failed him. Jeremiah had cause for resentment on several fronts. King Jehoiakim would not listen to his words. These, like all prophetic proclamations, were God's words for the sake of the people. His own villagers, as well as his family, felt he had dishonored them and wanted to kill him. "Not only his fellow villagers but even his extended family, his brothers and cousins, were in hot pursuit after him."[8] But even more, Jeremiah resented a God who, in his mind, had betrayed him. Jeremiah's efforts to forgive God exemplify the fourfold journey of forgiving.

Discovering the Injury

Jeremiah was called to be a prophet to the nation, called even before he was born. Yahweh encouraged him not to be afraid, that he would be guided in his speech and that Yahweh would be with him. "Have no fear before them, because I am with you to deliver you, says the LORD" (Jer 1:8).

So Jeremiah sets out to preach the message of God for all to hear. And, of course, he expects some backing. When Jeremiah is persecuted by the people and banished from their community life, he reminds God,

> When I found your words, I devoured them;
> they became my joy and the happiness of
> my heart,
> Because I bore your name,
> O LORD, God of hosts.
> I did not sit celebrating
> in the circle of merrymakers;
> Under the weight of your hand I sat alone
> because you filled me with indignation.
> Why is my pain continuous,
> my wound incurable, refusing to be healed?
> You have indeed become for me a treacherous
> brook,
> whose waters do not abide!
>
> —Jeremiah 15:16–18

In the beginning Jeremiah named his pain and railed in anger against God, who had failed to provide the promised support. This is an example of "unforgivable injury," an injury that shatters our concept of morality because a moral contract, a covenant, has been broken. Such an injury shatters our belief system and feels like betrayal.

Jeremiah experiences God as calling him to be an instrument, to speak a message to the people. But then God does not seem to support him in his call. In his "confessions" (11:18—12:6) Jeremiah cries out against God, whose help is lacking.

In discovering the injury, Jeremiah goes through Flanigan's forgiving process of naming, claiming, and blaming the injurer. Jeremiah "claims the injury" in his confessions of disappointment with God. Unmet expectations hurt, especially when they damage an intimate relationship with the One who "formed you in the womb . . . knew you . . . dedicated you, a prophet to the nations" (1:5). God, whom Jeremiah expects to be there for him in times of trouble, is not. Jeremiah is persecuted and imprisoned (37:15–16). Jeremiah puts the blame squarely on God and says, in so many words, *You, God, broke your covenant.* In other words: "God, you have been suing Israel for breach of contract, and I am your messenger in this regard. But when I undertook to be your messenger, you obligated yourself to defend me, and you have not followed through on your obligation. . . . I want to pass judgement upon you."[9] God responds to Jeremiah and promises to "balance the scales" with a visitation upon the men of Anatoth. Jeremiah attempts to "equalize the blame"; he "does not curse God, but curses the day he was born, which is to curse his call from God (1:5). He does not curse his mother but curses the day he was born, does not curse his father but curses the man who brought the news to his father of his birth."[10] This cursing phase helps Jeremiah, as it would anyone who has been injured, to claim the injury and place the blame.

Approaching Compassion

God, however, *is* with Jeremiah. God not only supports the prophet but shares his pain over the suffering of the people.

> My grief is incurable,
> my heart within me is faint.
> I am broken by the ruin of the daughter of my people.
> I am disconsolate; horror has seized me.
> —Jeremiah 8:18, 21

It is impossible to distinguish God from the prophet. They have become one in their compassion for the people. God and Jeremiah are also united in their frustration with a stubborn, willful people. God says,

> Would that I had in the desert
> a traveler's lodge!
> That I might leave my people
> and depart from them.
> —Jeremiah 9:1

Jeremiah's later laments turn into prayers of praise as he forgives apparent negligence: he sees that

> the LORD is with me, like a mighty champion:
> my persecutors will stumble, they will not triumph.
> —Jeremiah 20:11

Kathleen O'Connor applies the story of Jeremiah to all women today who "find their words rejected by religious authorities, their bodies battered, abused, wondering if God has abandoned and betrayed them."[11] Like many contemporary women, Jeremiah also survived his despair and continued to preach out of that "fire burning in my heart, imprisoned in my bones" (20:9), a fire that is greater than any human attempt to squelch it. This fire burning in our hearts is also greater than any image we may have of who God is or how God acts. For Jeremiah, God is personal and other, flexible and creative, compassionate and incomprehensible. For us, God may be these things and more. When we can accept a God without form and can live without a why, then we, too, have reached the point of compassion in our forgiving journey.

Choosing to Forgive

Ralph returned from his first singles support group meeting. The participants were people who had lost a spouse through death or divorce.

"How was it?" I asked.

"Well," he responded, "the divorcees were no fun to be with. They were filled with bitterness toward their former spouses. The widows and widowers were just angry at God!"

Ralph was insinuating that the latter group's situation is less complex and more easily resolved. Nevertheless, forgiveness requires a definite choice, whether one forgives another person or God. The process, intensity, and "side trips" of each forgiving journey vary with the wounded traveler. The choice to forgive is the choice for life. Through the prophet Jeremiah, God tells the exiles in Babylon, "Build houses to dwell in; plant gardens, and eat their fruits. Take wives and beget sons and daughters. . . . There you must increase in number, not decrease. Promote the welfare of the city to which I have exiled you; pray for it to the LORD, for upon its welfare depends your own" (29:5–7). This is an example of forgiving out of a sense of self-preservation; nevertheless, it is a choice for forgiveness. God promises a blessing, not a curse for the Israelites. "For I know well the plans I have in mind for you, says the LORD, plans for your welfare, not for woe! plans to give you a future full of hope" (29: 11). Jeremiah argues and struggles with God, but in his heart he has chosen God.

> You would be in the right, O LORD,
> if I should dispute with you;
> even so, I must discuss the case with you.
> Why does the way of the godless prosper,
> why live all the treacherous in contentment?
> . . .
> You, O Lord, know me, you see me,
> you have found that at heart I am with you.
> —Jeremiah 12:1, 3

Jeremiah has a passion for God, struggles with God, flees and returns to the One who, although accused by Jeremiah of desertion, has never really left him.

Seeing Anew

Jeremiah is transformed by letting go of his accusation of desertion. He is renewed by God, who has been trying to say to him, and to Israel, all along:

> With age-old love I have loved you;
> so I have kept my mercy toward you.
> Again I will restore you and you shall be rebuilt.
> —Jeremiah 31:3–4

God renews God's commitment to the people:

> But this is the covenant which I will make with the house of Israel after those days, says the LORD. I will place my law within them, and write it upon their hearts; I will be their God, and they shall be my people. No longer will they have need to teach their friends and kinsmen how to know the LORD. All, from least to greatest, shall know me, says the LORD, for I will forgive their evildoing and remember their sin no more. (Jer 31:33–34)

In transformation, the final step in the forgiving process, we see anew with the eyes of wisdom, with the heart of God. Carroll Stuhlmueller summarizes this process in the life of Jeremiah by pointing out:

> If the person of Jeremiah is the prophetic message, then we must deal with a person who paradoxically combines exceptional obedience to God with vigorous argumentation against God (12:1), who struggles with doubt and anger, and at times succumbs to them, only to rise purified and transformed (9:1; 15:19). . . . We find the message of Jeremiah reverberates in our own lives, as we struggle and fall and rise, as we agonize and flee and return. The name for this is that of Jeremiah himself: *The Lord rises* in our collapse, to show that the new life is God's more than our own.[12]

Jeremiah reveals a God who teaches us numerous ways to forgive. Like God, we can forgive without placing demands or requiring recompense. Payment, atonement, has already been made by Jesus. "All in all, no one in the history of Israel was more like Jesus than Jeremiah."[13] Both wept with compassion over their people. Both were rejected by them, suffered, and died. Through them, the people experienced resurrection.

THE TEACHING OF JESUS

It is at times difficult for us, as it was for Job and Jeremiah, to believe that this incomprehensible God bestows blessings upon us rather than curses. God's ways go far beyond the parameters of both biblical and contemporary culture, which look to God to reward good and punish evil. Instead, all creation, the person next to us, and the very breath we breathe are signs of God's loving desire that we may "have life and have it more abundantly" (Jn 10:10). Like the rain, which falls on the just and unjust alike, fullness of life is promised to all. That promise is solidified by the knowledge that we are forgiven and can forgive. God tells us through the prophet Isaiah,

> I have brushed away your offenses like a cloud,
> your sins like a mist;
> return to me, for I have redeemed you.
> —Isaiah 44:22

We imitate God, whose unconditional love and forgiveness say to us, "Be kind to one another, compassionate, forgiving one another as God has forgiven you in Christ" (Eph 4:32). God teaches us to pray: "Forgive us our debts as we forgive our debtors" (Mt 6:12). We have a storytelling God who presents us with the parable of the Prodigal Son (Lk 15:11–32) to show us that unconditional loving is possible. Forgiving without demand, condition, or repentance is conceivable. Enright points out "that although the son thought about his repentant words before meeting his father, he did not have a chance to say them when his father, upon seeing him from a distance, was filled with compassion."[14] It is this compassionate, loving, forgiving God to whom we shout, "Show me, O LORD, your way!" (Ps 27:11).

Jesus portrays God as "free and gracious . . . not to be controlled by Israel's . . . boundaries."[15] God as presented by the gospels, the good news, is near to us, compassionate; God loves without limit. Jesus is our primary teacher of forgiving. A "prevailing theme in the authentic Jesus material of the Gospels is an emphasis on reconciliation and forgiveness at the expense of judgment or retribution."[16] The New Testament contains many passages about forgiveness.[17] These references demonstrate that the ministry of Jesus was one of

> transformation and forgiveness. . . . The Greek term for forgiveness, *Aphesis*, has the connotation of "release," a freedom from bondage of sin. The Lucan Jesus not only directly forgives sins, as in the cases of the paralytic (Lk. 5:20), the "woman of the city" (Lk. 7:47–48), and his own executioners (Lk. 23:34), but he "releases" those bound with the physical burdens of pain and illness, which the biblical mind recognized as the legacy of sin. The care of the woman bent double, found only in (Lk. 13:10–17), is typical of this liberating dimension of forgiveness.[18]

Following the gospel means learning to forgive. Jesus is an extraordinary teacher in this regard. His lessons included initiating forgiveness, confronting sin, and canceling debt, all while maintaining each person's dignity. "In the end, all forgivers do as Jesus did: they restore self-worth to the offender; they cancel a debt; they confer freedom; and they love beyond their imagining"[19]—and beyond their images! Old images of God are exploded by Job and Jeremiah. Jesus expands our God-horizons beyond the stars. Jesus is a teacher of truth, a preacher of the good news, hope for the sinner, and healer of the broken-hearted.

According to Morton Kelsey, "One of the reasons why modern Christians do not understand Jesus is that they think of Him as a university professor of ethics rather than a shaman."[20] By reading the gospels with an eye to the activity of Jesus, we see that he teaches primarily with the example of his life. As Walter Brueggemann writes, "The staggering works of Jesus—feeding, healing, casting out, forgiving—happened not to those who held to the old order but to those who yearned because the old order had failed them or squeezed them out."[21]

The teachings and parables were reflections upon Jesus' life by the community of believers. The faith of these believers also altered their God images, and that process of revelation continues to unfold among us.

CONCLUSION

Forgiving can be unconditional only if it finds its source in the life of God. This dimension, like the very concept of God, is beyond our imagination. We have witnesses, however, that there is a need for the healing power of forgiving. And Jesus teaches us that forgiving unconditionally is a possibility, a way we share in the life of God. There is hope in healing. The power to forgive is ours to use. It is a gift of grace, given so that we can have life and have it to the full.

There is healing in forgiving—for the wounded one, for the perpetrator or the perceived perpetrator, and for the world itself. "The forgiveness task is all encompassing; that is, we learn to forgive not only ourselves and others, but life itself and, by implication, the Intelligence that is the Source of Life."[22] Ultimately, when all is said and done, all is forgiven. When all is said and done and all is forgiven, we see God.

3

A Theological Reflection on Forgiving

Receive the Holy Spirit.
Whose sins you forgive are forgiven them,
and whose sins you retain are retained.
—John 20:22–23

A Question of Authority

According to the Hebrew scriptures, only God can forgive. Therefore people were scandalized with Jesus when he told the paralytic, "Courage, child, your sins are forgiven" (Mt 9:2). The scribes thought he was blaspheming. Jesus understood their thinking and said, "But that you may know that the Son of Man has authority on earth to forgive sins—he then said to the paralytic, 'Rise, pick up your stretcher, and go home'" (9:6). In *Jesus*, Edward Schillebeeckx explains why the Jewish apocalyptical tradition holds the forgiveness of sins as God's exclusive right. The high priest could *declare* a person free of sin, but only God could forgive sin.[1] William Klassen carries this discussion to the power of the priest:

> Forgiveness thus is seen not as something God alone declares but as a process that he carries out through his community on earth and that finds its ultimate ratification in heaven. If the Jews were scandalized that Jesus of Nazareth would say to a man, "Your sins are forgiven," and accuse him of blasphemy, how much more would they be scandalized to hear that a group of people exercised the privilege of forgiving people their sins? It is a moving tribute to the power of the early church that they did not shrink from this great responsibility and an indication of our weakness that we have so often returned to the notion that only God can forgive sins.[2]

God lives in us and shares life with us. We learn from and partake in God's power. This is a forgiving God, the psalmist reminds us:

> We are overcome by our sins;
> it is you who pardon them.
> —Psalm 65:4

All of us share in the power to forgive, as given to the church by Jesus. Through baptism we "priestly people" are invited to share in God's power of unconditional loving and forgiving. We have the power to forgive the wrongs done to us and thereby release—or cling to—accompanying resentment. But have we abdicated our power to forgive by confusing forgiveness with reconciliation? While related, the two are not the same. Forgiving is essential to the sacrament of reconciliation. Reconciliation may or may not follow upon forgiving.

It is to be hoped that reclamation of our personal power to forgive will lead us to fuller appreciation of the sacrament of reconciliation as the communal celebration of that power. This sacrament may well be for our culture a hidden treasure of grace, healing, peace, and spiritual growth. Tradition reminds us that the sacrament has a dual purpose: to forgive sin, and to bring us the healing power of God's grace to guide us in our daily lives.[3]

In the Catholic tradition, John 20:22–23 is seen as the origin of the priest's power, in the name of God, to forgive sin during the sacrament of reconciliation. However, according to Bruce Vawter, "it is equally true that the Church's power over sin is also exercised in Baptism and the preaching of the redemptive word."[4] It seems Raymond Brown disagrees when he says, "As for the power to forgive or hold sins, there is nothing in the text itself that associates forgiveness with either preaching the Gospel or admission to Baptism."[5] Brown reminds us that the Council of Trent, in reaction to Protestant reformers, condemned the proposition that this power was offered to each of Christ's followers. Brown maintains that "this verse should be understood as the power exercised by ordained priests in the Sacrament of Penance."[6]

Brown's view is representative of what most Catholics believe. Yet sacraments not only confer grace, in and of themselves, but they are the public confirmation of what is already happening in the Christian community. The sacrament of matrimony, for example, celebrates bonds of love that already exist. Eucharist nourishes the community that has gathered around the table. The sacrament of reconciliation celebrates forgiveness experienced between persons and in the person-God relationship. Forgiveness, as we have seen, is not the same as reconciliation. Forgiving is a personal, private affair of the heart. By forgiving, a relationship has changed. That is cause for rejoicing. When reconciliation also happens, it is cause for celebration.

Forgiving creates the possibility for reconciliation by the very fact that it has happened. The parable of the Prodigal Son (Lk 15:11–32) is as much the story of compassion on the part of the father as it is of repentance on the part of the son. Christian Duquoc writes: "Forgiveness creates a new relationship: the offending past itself becomes positive; the circle of 'rights' is broken. All definitive reconciliation requires that the circle of judgment should be broken."[7]

If reunion is appropriate, it can be celebrated publicly in the sacrament of reconciliation. Duquoc continues:

> The sacramental symbol should make clear that forgiveness is a social function necessary to our history as it makes its way towards reconciliation; that particular reconciliations are a promise of the total reconciliation that is impossible as things are now; and that enmity between men has a source which can only be understood in the light of the Christian revelation of sin and the opposition to God.[8]

Forgiveness is personal. Reconciliation is interpersonal. Both are social in their effects.

Brown summarizes his position by saying:

> We doubt that there is sufficient evidence to confine the power of forgiving and holding of sin, granted in Jn. 20:23, to a specific exercise of power in the Christian community, whether that be admission to Baptism or forgiveness in Penance. These are but partial manifestations of a much larger power, namely, the power to isolate, repel, and negate evil

> and sin, a power given to Jesus in his mission by the Father and given in turn by Jesus though the Spirit to those whom he commissions.[9]

With this last sentence, Brown reiterates his previous position and the tradition of the church, saying it is those called to priesthood who are "commissioned" by Jesus to exercise this larger power. Scripture assures us that God's healing power has been granted. Tradition teaches us the way a particular community exercises that power. Theological reflection comes about by bridging scripture and tradition over the river of life. To be Catholic today is to be about bridge building. Priestly power to forgive sin in the name of God is not denied. The power given the church, as the community of believers, to forgive or retain injury is an aspect of forgiveness that needs attention in our time.

Love is bigger than our wounds. God, who is love, has given each of us a share in that love, in that life, in the power of forgiving. The fact that we forgive by the grace of God makes the timing unique to the person and the situation. That we do so in union with God assures us that human freedom and integrity will be respected. George Aschenbrenner states: "If the forgiving love of God is to reconcile an individual's heart and a whole community, it will require both time and the careful cooperation of believing persons. God's reconciling forgiveness never happens to us all at once nor in utter disregard of our own dispositions."[10]

A woman named Jenny is still working to forgive her abusive father:

As a child Jenny was abused by her father. The abuse was followed by neglect. After discovering that he had been molesting Jenny, her mother said, "If you touch her again, I will leave you." As a result, Jenny's father did not touch her again; as a matter of fact, he avoided her. Jenny came to feel neglected, that he did not love her. As an adult, Jenny thought she had forgiven her father—that is, until last September, when she dreamed of her grandparents in heaven, smiling and holding her three babies whom she had miscarried. Missing from the picture was her father, who by this time had also died. Someone asked her if she had allowed him to be there. Maybe she really had not forgiven him and was still punishing him. In a subsequent dream he appeared in the picture but was in the background looking over their shoulders. She asked herself, will he ever be able to be fully part of the picture? She looked at me, rather sadly, and said, "I don't think I'd trust him to hold my babies just yet."

God's reconciling forgiveness, as one aspect of God's grace, is available to us step by step, bit by bit, as we are ready to receive it into our hearts.

THE NATURE OF SIN

Theological reflection on forgiveness requires an exploration of the nature and meaning of sin. How is sin operative in creation? According to Paul Ricoeur, "The etiological myth of Adam is the most extreme attempt to separate the origin of evil from the origin of good: its intention is to set up a 'radical' origin of evil distinct from the more 'primordial' origin of the goodness of things."[11] Creation was good, yet somehow evil came into being. We now live in a state of unfulfillment. However, evil is not necessarily sin. Evil may be a situation or event that negatively affects our life; sin involves decision-making and choice. Edward Farley points out that "differentiating sin from the tragic is one of the seminal insights of the Hebraic tradition."[12]

What, then, is sin? Loretta Dornisch explains:

> Sin may be viewed positively or negatively. Some ways of expressing sin as nothingness are: loss of a bond; missing the target; being on a tortuous road; rebelling; being lost. . . . This experience of nothingness was compensated by the motif of pardon-return. The concept of sin as something positive perdured even in the prophets. . . . There is a binding force of sin, a spirit of wickedness, which cannot be reduced to the subjective or individual dimension. This symbolism is countered by the symbolism of redemption: buying back, freeing, liberating.[13]

According to Farley, "The very essence of sin . . . is to fail to acknowledge the sovereign as sovereign, and to repudiate the subject to master relation."[14] Sin, in this framework, is idolatry; it is choosing someone or something other than God to be god in our lives. Sin is a matter of will, and it is experienced both personally and communally.

The classical view of evil sees the essence of sin as rebellion or pride. Farley shows that this view, though insightful, has problems. The concept of sin is legitimately put to question in light of contemporary rejection of arbitrary rules and the awareness of psychological influences on our behavior. In response to his own question, "Whatever became of sin?" Karl Menninger writes: "I believe there is 'sin' which is expressed in ways which cannot be subsumed under verbal artifacts such as 'crime,' 'disease,' 'delinquency,' 'deviancy.' There *is* unethical behavior; there *is* wrongdoing."[15]

There is sin, but the voice of women in describing its nature has been notably absent from our religious history. Judith Plaskow says that the "framework" for sin as "pride" is a masculine paradigm that does not consider the experience of women. She suggests:

> The "sin" which the feminine role in modern society creates and encourages in women is not illegitimate self-centeredness but failure to center the self, the failure to take responsibility for one's own life. It could be said that women's sin, so far from being the sin of pride, lies in leaving the sin of pride to men.[16]

Sin can be seen as pride, power, or other forms of self-aggrandizement, self-diminishment, and self-abnegation. Basically, each makes God a "displaced person." Whether we experience sin in the secret recesses of our hearts, or as consequence of another's action, each is a form of idolatry. Whether sin is spoken of in classical or contemporary language, whether it is seen from a female or male perspective, the effect is the same: damage. The one who forgives knows evil by name. The one who forgives is empowered by the ever present grace of God to do some renaming.

A MATTER OF WILL

Forgiveness is "neither natural, instinctive, nor logical."[17] So what makes it happen?

While driving out to seeing her dying father, Mary Alice prayed, "Whatever you are or have been, or have done to me, I forgive you." The night after her father died she had a vision—she knew it was not a dream because she was awake. She was in the corner in a fetal position. A bright light shone around her. A man wearing a red robe came to her, opened his arms, and embraced her. She heard the words, "Choose life." Mary Alice had a feeling of unconditional love and assurance that things would be all right.

Three years later Mary Alice is still working out the details of forgiving her father, her husband, herself, and God. But the first step was taken with the choice to forgive her father.

Doris Donnelly writes, "You need not determine a precise strategy or even see its actual possibility. All you need to do is decide that this is what you will do."[18] That decision sets us on a path and opens our heart to that moment of grace when forgiveness happens. Hugh Ross Mackintosh, one of the early twentieth century's most influential Scottish theologians, concurs:

> As we encounter or practise it in human affairs, forgiveness is an active process in the mind and temper of a wronged person, by means of which he abolishes a moral hindrance to fellowship with the wrong-doer, and re-establishes the freedom and happiness of friendship.[19]

When we decide to forgive, we choose not to be confined to the pain, anger, fear, and resentment of the past. Forgiving frees us of the double jeopardy of negative consequences added to the pain of the original wound. Forgiving opens up a new way of being and of relating—for the sake of a healthy self and for personal and social transformation. To release another of our rightful resentment is not easy; it requires courage and a conscious, rational choice. When we choose to forgive, we release the injurer from the ties that bound us through the wound. We even choose, as Flanigan says, to "relinquish any remaining illusions" that we can "require the injurer to pay off some debt."[20]

David, a young pastor, felt the senior pastor at his previous assignment had "done him in." Whenever David needed to blame someone or take out his anger on someone, the face of the senior pastor came before his mind's eye. It took years for David to choose to let go of the comfort of having someone to blame and to assume responsibility for his own life—to forgive.

Jesus, our teacher par excellence of unconditional forgiveness,

> is not naive, he does not ask us to be passive, he does not require us to give up fighting against evil but he shows that equivalence in evil, even in the name of justice, does not transform human society. What is required is an attitude that is not determined by what has already been done, an innovative, creative gesture.[21]

This gesture is unconditional regard for the injurer, the essence of forgiveness.

The choice to forgive is the choice for new life. It is a decision to live life to the full. Virgil Elizondo writes, "Jesus broke the cycle of offense for offense and thus initiated radical and new possibilities for the human person, for human relations, and for society at large."[22] The choice to forgive is the option to rework the script for our life's story.

THE MOMENT OF GRACE

Today grace is often understood as God's life in us urging us to change (*metanoia*) and to transform. It is a liberating, life-giving influence. The message of grace is basically the good—old—news that God is with us. It includes the "incredible claim that in light of the incarnation, the divine and the human while distinct, are not separate."[23] This is comforting theology. It is in keeping with the message of connectedness and interdependence preached by feminists, mystics, and ecological theologians. It is the promise of our God. The presence of God is reserved not only for the human person but given to all nature. It is obsolete to distinguish between nature and grace. There is no such thing as "ungraced nature." As Elizabeth Dreyer affirms, "The depth of the cosmos is graced irrevocably by the Incarnation and available to everyone all the time. In other words, there's nowhere else to live except in a graced world."[24]

The power of God being with us, being one with us, enables us to break the cycle of evil and not pass on the pain. "The pattern of sin is stopped when people, by the grace of God, imitate Jesus in not becoming carriers of the contagion . . . do not allow the sins visited on them to control their attitudes and behavior toward others."[25] The lives of ordinary persons doing extraordinary things bear witness to God's grace.

One such person is Corrie ten Boom. After preaching about forgiveness at a church service in Munich, ten Boom tells of seeing a former S.S. guard from Ravensbruck, the Nazi concentration camp where she and her sister were interred during World War II. Corrie recalls:

> His hand was thrust out to shake mine. And I, who had preached so often to the people in Bloemendaal the need to forgive, kept my hand at my side.
>
> Even as the angry, vengeful thoughts boiled through me, I saw the sin of them. Jesus Christ had died for this man; was I going to ask for more? Lord Jesus, I prayed, forgive me and help me to forgive him.
>
> I tried to smile, I struggled to raise my hand. I could not. I felt nothing, not the slightest spark of warmth or charity. And so again I breathed a silent prayer. Jesus, I cannot forgive him. Give me Your forgiveness.
>
> As I took his hand the most incredible thing happened. From my shoulder along my arm and through my hand a current seemed to pass from me to him, while into my heart sprang a love for this stranger that almost overwhelmed me.

> And so I discovered that it is not on our forgiveness any more than on our goodness that the world's healing hinges, but on His. When He tells us to love our enemies, He gives, along with the command, the love itself.[26]

God does not leave us alone on our forgiving journey. God is with us, shares life with us in the process. " How?" we might ask. We know that it is, but what is this "grace of God" that allows persons even in the most dire circumstances to exhibit extraordinary human greatness?

Dornisch calls grace "excess" and "superabundance," reminding us that "a logic of equivalence emphasizes sin, death, and a limited idea of law, while on the other side, a logic of superabundance calls for justice, grace and life."[27] Rahner speaks of grace as God's self-communication. He says it is "habitual" in the sense that "God's supernatural self-communication is permanently offered," and that it is "actual" insofar as it "actually sustains the act whereby it is accepted."[28] He says this self-communication of God, "both as given, and as accepted by man, is essentially God's free, personal uncovenanted favor."[29] Rahner also notes that "grace may be experienced in the most diverse forms . . . unutterable joy, unconditional love, unconditional obedience, a feeling of loving unity with the 'world.'"[30]

Judy felt hurt and betrayed when the pastor of a large parish did not renew her contract. She found it impossible to attend that church without a resurgence of anger and pain. She started going to another parish. It took her six months to be able to make the choice even to try to forgive. Each time she prayed "forgive us our trespasses, as we forgive those who trespass against us," she would add, "some day." Judy realized, three months later, that she had left out the "some day" addition to her prayer. She no longer needed it. "I realized that I did forgive. The pain is still there, but it no longer matters." There was a smile on her face as she spoke.

As Klassen says, "Forgiveness occurs . . . only as you yourself participate in the power of God to forgive and as you allow that power to work through you."[31] Grace is the gift of God's loving presence, God's life with us, offered to every person. We are to accept or to reject that presence, that grace, free to forgive and be compassionate as our God is compassionate.

Writing: A Theological Reflection Process

Our thinking about God, our teaching about how God relates to the universe, and the meaning of God in our lives are expressed in our writing. Good writing helps people imagine what a gospel-governed world would be. It provides opportunity for another way of looking at our lives. I have discovered that before I articulate my theology, certain things need to happen. The rituals and preparations I find essential for writing can be adapted to storytelling, teaching, and preaching as well.

The first step is to study. Read the readings. Do the exegetical work. Gather insights from the scholars, and promptly place them on the back burner. Consider your readers. What are their strengths? What moves them? What cultural and educational language do they speak? What are their struggles, losses, needs, blind spots? Reread the scriptures and pertinent materials.

The second step is to center. Giving yourself time and space allows the message meant for these people to percolate from the scripture through you. The centering may take several days; you may need the patience to "sleep on it."

Often the message comes unexpectedly—upon awakening, in the shower, during a walk, in prayer, or even while talking to someone on the phone.

Third, experience the void as you approach your notebook or face an empty computer screen. Prayer, waiting, trust, and tolerating the impasse before creativity characterize this moment. The scripture itself contains the chaos and provides the focus for the message. Stillness sifts the myriad of books read, needs seen, and possible approaches. The Spirit hovers over creation now as much as on the first day.

Fourth, imbibe the word and live seeing everything in light of its message. Writing comes from the inside out. The written word that is comprehended by the reader comes from the heart. As the scripture inside you looks for expression, you see someone in need, walk along a lake, converse with a friend, through filters of compassion. You long to make the connection between inner contemplation and outer experience. In writing, you become the bridge between the message and the people, the vehicle through whom divine loving is articulated.

Fifth, realize that purification is a necessary step before writing or speaking a word that is of God for the sake of the people. You have labored, but it is not your work. Prayer, fasting, and ritual cleansing allow you to let go of ego gratification, attachment to certain outcomes, or feelings of self-glorification. Focus on the message.

Sixth, subsequent transformation is probably more for the author than the readers. You cannot write, go through a process of absorbing a message from our loving, compassionate God, and not be altered. As a writer you see with new eyes, have learned to trust the spirit working within you, and are filled with desire to share the fruits of your labor.

Seven, you reintegrate the message for yourself and the readers appropriate the message of the writing for their own lives. Ideally, both see with new eyes and live in a new way. Corrie ten Boom integrated the message of her preaching, teaching, and writing on forgiveness when, with the grace of God, she could shake the hand of a former oppressor. God gave her the grace and the strength and the love, but ten Boom did not cease asking for it!

Eight, let go by destroying the writing. By consciously reincorporating the message of the writing into your life, the work itself no longer has meaning. This is why the book comes to have a life of its own beyond the author. I have files of chapter drafts, and they are memorabilia of moments of divine encounters along life's way with God. Writing is a privilege because it allows you to enter into correspondence with God for the sake of the people. Writing is theologizing; it is articulating your discoveries about God and creation. Writing is a work of compassion because it empowers you to see with the eyes of the heart. Writing gives you the gift of time to embrace God's word and God's people, hugging them both to your heart. In the process, you are altered.

Conclusion

Remember Desert Storm? That military action spawned much theological reflection on the nature of personal and communal sin. Because of our national desert experience, renewed significance was given to desert stories. Desert stories appear to be success stories: the struggle is won, temptation is overcome, the enemy is conquered. Desert stories, images, and symbols abound in scripture and in our world. The Hebrew people did reach the Promised Land, albeit after a forty-year journey. Jesus was led into the desert, where he triumphed over the devil's temptations.

And we, as a nation, conquered our "desert enemy" by storm!

But are there desert stories of failure? Do we ever tell of succumbing to temptation? Are we ever defeated by the enemy? Those are the desert stories buried deep in our hearts, often hidden from our awareness.

Our personal desert stories may relate vulnerabilities of spirit we call sin. We give in to the temptation of pride when we think we know what someone else needs, and more, when we see ourselves as the answer to that need. We fail to triumph over our personal evil or arrogance when we see ourselves as right or as having power over another. There are as many personal desert stories as there are persons. When they come to light, all we can say is, "Lord, have mercy."

Collectively, we have desert failures as well. When we think we have defeated an "enemy," when we have used violence in the name of righteousness, when we have succumbed to the temptation of dehumanizing those we have overpowered—as when we speak of "collateral damage" rather than human casualties or victims of war—when in our collective imagination we have become the Almighty, we have sinned and cry out, "Christ, have mercy."

Victorious or wounded, we come through a desert experience altered. The Hebrews found a home and let go of a nomadic way of life. Jesus was tried, tested, comforted, and strengthened to begin his ministry; he could no longer be just the son of the carpenter from Nazareth. The Iraqi people were devastated, the Kuwaiti people, euphoric. The allied forces of Desert Storm would have to live a long time with the consequences of this brief "action." Victorious or wounded, we come through a desert experience needing the ministry of angels. We are overwhelmed and moan, "Lord, have mercy."

Our personal and collective desert stories have another dimension too: the presence of a loving, forgiving God. God provides us with milk, honey, and manna in our desert and nourishes us back to life. God is a lover of life who makes the desert bloom, heals our wounded hearts, and restores our faith in one another by encouraging us to look at others, as ourselves. God is creator of the universe whose Spirit hovers over creation. God is totally in love with creation and invites us to be so, as well. It is God alone who can lead us out of the desert, God alone who gives us new life and hope, God alone who constantly beckons us so God does not have to do this all alone!

4

Forgiving as a Family Affair

Exploring the Roots

Fran moaned, and for a third time that night awoke with excruciating pain in her upper right jaw. For the last three years, chewing on the right side of her mouth had been impossible. She had seen the dentist several times, and x-rays of her sinuses revealed nothing unusual.

For a "wise woman" of fifty, distress is itself very distressing! Fran drove many hours each month to care for aging parents. Her father's chronic and dramatic illness, her own life being "on hold," and her mother's need for support aroused anger and resentment in her heart. She took it out on her teeth and clenched them tight.

At the beginning of August, Fran returned to her hometown to be near her parents. By the end of the month she'd had a root canal. The root canal became a symbol, a call to attend to the source of her pain. It meant finding a way back to the beginning of the pain in order to create a path for expelling the poison. Only by means of such a penetrating examination can healing occur.

Healing family pain requires just such intenseness as we look at the pain that has its source in a wounded root. Venturing through the roots of a family system calls for extreme patience, for we sit with an open wound. Clearing out the findings may bring to light family secrets that have greatly affected the way we deal with relationships, unconsciously causing isolation, alienation, anxiety, and division of loyalties among family members and across generations. Larry Graham writes, "A family secret is one or more events that affect the family, including the psychological status of individuals of the family, without acknowledgment or accountability."[1]

Bringing family secrets to light is not synonymous with indiscriminately hanging out the family's "dirty laundry." Everything need not be told to all, in the same way, for healing to happen. Honesty, discretion, and wisdom are crucial in confrontation. We do not seek to make amends directly when doing so would cause further injury to the person or others.

Families are the environment in which caring is expected, growth is smiled upon, and creativity either challenged or stifled. In the family, our primary community, forgiving becomes a means to new life and non-forgiving an occasion for building up resentment and anger, which lead to further negative consequences. Our negative feelings are complicated by the fact that each one of us also carries within us the unfinished business of previous generations. In this chapter we will see some of the effects of non-forgiving and explore the meaning of forgiveness and its implications for the family system. I believe forgiving is healing for the soul.

Forgiving is also healing for the system in that it alters negative patterns of behavior and demeaning relationships. The forgiving process in a family reminds me of the root canal. The system is changed from the inside out. The infection is cleared out, and the dentist can begin to rebuild the tooth structure. In forgiving, the body—the family—can again function according to its nature. And that is *good*!

Alla Bozath-Campbell writes, "Pain is always a symptom of some injury, an illness or a woundedness. . . . Paradoxically, the way past the pain is to go all the way through it."[2] Forgiving and being forgiven alter our lives and effect healing among our loved ones.

FAMILY STORIES

A family includes multiple generations of people who have lifelong commitments to one another through ties of blood or law. A family is a system. It is organic. It is, to varying degrees, healthy or dysfunctional. Individuals are part of that whole and affect and are affected by family life. I also consider a community, defined here as a group of adults connected not by blood but by commitment, as family.

Developmental tasks that we need to accomplish as members of a family, include processing the pain inherited from our families, giving and receiving forgiveness, letting go of attachments, and living in hope of a future life. It is my belief that these tasks are completed in us while we are on earth; we work through them, one way or another, before death.

Conversations at the Doorway

Mary Ellen was a Dominican sister. She was a generous community member. After thirty years of teaching high school mathematics, Mary Ellen retired to take care of a grade school library and manage local community and province finances. Then she got sick. I happened to be the one who took her to the doctor and was with her when he explained the test results. She had cancer of the pancreas, with about six months to live. It was the beginning of the last stage of her courageous journey toward the next life. Mary Ellen allowed me to accompany her part of the way on this final journey. Following are snippets of our conversations and my reflections during the last days of her life.

> *March 9.* We received a call from the hospital. You had about two hours to live. The community gathered, and each sister said her personal goodbye. We sang the "Hail, Holy Queen," our custom for a dying sister. We waited. You did not die. The community sang in English, Latin, and Swahili, and still you did not die. We prayed psalms, thanked you for your life, and encouraged you in your journey to the next life. You did not die. Knowing you did not want to be alone at the time of death, we decided to keep an around-the-clock vigil.
>
> *March 11.* My turn to sit with you came again two days later. The last words I remembered hearing from you were "Lord, deliver me," as they came to change your bed and turn you again. Your sense of pride was still with you. Stella and I now sat on each side of your bed holding a hand that responded to the touch.
>
> *March 14.* Today you were given a more powerful dose of morphine. The doctor said, "Let's keep her comfortable and forget trying to transport her to the Villa [our nursing facility]. It won't be long."
>
> Then, he addressed you, saying, "Hi, sister!"

For the first time in days, you opened your eyes wide, smiled, and said, "Hi, doctor."

"How are you?" he asked.

"Just fine, thank you." Your response was as clear as a bell.

March 15. I had a dream last night. Someone had been taking things little by little. Most of the dream was spent playing detective and trying to figure out who was the thief. I was a parent of two or three children. The oldest son came home, to a bare house inside and out. I said, "Who took all this?" He replied, "I did. I've ordered all new furniture for you. It's on its way! Remember, I told you that?" I realized he had been taking little things with each trip to clear out the house and make it easier to move the new furniture in.

I connected this dream with you, Mary Ellen. You had already given away all your treasured possessions. Thus, "taking things" referred to your physical diminishment. Your body was now the size of a child's, your glasses had been removed, and we were to witness the loss of speech, hearing, touch, and finally, breath. Only then could you move into your new home.

March 16. Mary Ellen, you said, "I have work to do . . . before the end . . . I'm afraid." I prayed Psalm 23. You seemed comforted and relaxed a little.

March 17. You talked all day. I mean, continually. You mumbled mostly, but I could discern words like, "I'm not ready yet. . . . I don't understand. . . . Why is this happening to me? . . . I believe in God." Later, I heard you say, "What I really want to do is get off the bed and stand by the people." How could you have known that yesterday's gospel was the story of Jesus healing the paralytic and saying to him, "Courage, child, your sins are forgiven. . . . Rise, pick up your stretcher, and go home" (Mt 9:2, 6). Was your faith as strong as the paralytic's in the story? Were you receiving your own healing? That evening I was allowed to listen in on what seemed to be a great dialogue between God and you. Phrases I could comprehend were, "Let me get out of this damn thing. . . . Are we taken care of? . . . Oh, God, help us and save us. . . . I want my rights. . . . Let me get out of here. . . . Let's put this thing in the grave!"

March 18. I sat here, just looking at you and realizing that it has been one week since we got the call that you had only two hours to live. Mary Ellen, you are ineffable! You struggle and resign yourself as you engage in the timeless mystery of living and letting go, a mystery that is as real as your labored breathing in and breathing out. You baffle medical science. You have been on your "death bed" for almost two weeks. Doctors and nurses have begun to refrain from using scientific terms and now speak the language of the spirit. At the very moment I was thinking to myself, What else are you working on? What are you trying to teach us? you asked aloud, "What are we meant to see?" Do dying persons have a heightened sense of perception? Can they read the hearts of those around them? Then you said, clear as day, "Come, girls, let me go."

That evening I sat by your bed and held your hand. You gathered your strength and pulled my hand up to your lips and kissed it. You said, "Beauty . . . duty . . . tell them all about it."

To be sure I understood what you meant, I asked, "You want me to tell?"

You responded, "Yes."

I said, "You are teaching us. I'll try to tell them all about it."

You slept for a while, then awoke with a start and said, "I'm going out on the boat."

I responded, "Yes, you are taking the boat to the other side."

"I'm going around the world."

I ventured a guess, "I bet your spirit is going around the world to say goodbye before going to the other world."

It did not surprise me when, months later, I heard other sisters tell about sitting with dying ones who talked of "being at the edge of the earth." You had already covered that lesson!

As you tightened your weak grip on my hand, I said, "Let God work things out in you."

"That's what I'm trying to do," you responded, with more patience toward my pious remarks than I would have had.

I stayed with you through the night. At one point you turned your head slightly, looked at me, and said, "You fight!"

I answered, "Yes, I'll fight. You let go."

The conversation was then interspersed with moans and groans, delirium and pain. Once in a while, you voiced clear statements, such as, "Can you understand me? . . . I've got to give it up. . . . You got yourself in for more than you bargained for. . . . I know the way out. . . . I see your body up there."

The words "trust the way out" came from my mouth. I do not know where the words came from, but they were exactly right.

Reminiscent of St. Paul's statement that words cannot describe the glory that awaits those who love God, you said, "If you could see what I see. . . . Everything is where it shouldn't be."

I told you to rest, but your response was, "Really, I've got to tell you all this." As with any mystical experience, you wanted to tell but could not find the words.

"Things were left unseasoned, so they were left—if you ask me. . . . Is this day one?" you asked.

"Yes, it is day one."

Mary Ellen, a shy, quiet woman, had been talking constantly from March 17 until March 19, the feast of St. Joseph. A nurse said, "There is something she hasn't said." I felt this was a narration of a person's life story, reflection upon it, and settlement of unresolved issues. How much related to the need to forgive and be forgiven I do not know. We do know that unresolved issues are transmitted along generations. I believe Mary Ellen broke the cycle and healed much familial pain through her own suffering. At one point she said, "In the evaluation, I am too valuable. . . . I'm upset with my mother . . . the fire . . . my mother needs to be gotten out of there and I can't do anything. . . . It's all got to be taken care of. . . . I need to worry about this life . . . my mother . . . to help . . . I never knew all this stuff." Is this the babble of a delirious woman or the insight into and final analysis of a life resolved? When Mary Ellen was a child, the family home burned down and her mother was almost killed in the fire. Her parents were both killed in a car accident when she was about twelve.

March 20. You died at 8:54 P.M., Mary Ellen. Your body looked like Rembrandt's painting "Death." Heat radiated from your shoulder, where I had my hand. I felt the warmth for a long time after the doctor said, "You don't need me to tell you what you know. She is dead." Your spirit remained with us for a long time and peace filled the room. Mystics speak about the body being in the soul. People today talk about a person's aura or radiance. Physicists explain the significance of energy fields. You, Mary Ellen, taught me that the soul is not in the body, the body is in the soul. I touched your body and was embraced

> by your soul. The effect was deep, abiding peace. One sister recalled that yesterday you looked at something afar, started smiling, and said, "Gorgeous!" Then you laughed and said, "Beautiful!" It seems you had glimpses of what was to come. Today is the first day of spring. We had our first spring rain. The buds are out. It is a good day to begin new life.
>
> Thank you for allowing us to walk you part of the way home. We who accompany one another in life and in death are also reborn. As we become the coaches in a re-birthing room, saying "Let go. . . . Go home," we find ourselves in possession of new life. You gave Stella, Kathleen, and me the gift of being present at the moment of your re-birthing. Thank you. I will tell others. I live confident in the fact that issues do get resolved, healing is possible, there is hope. I have seen that patience, long-suffering, peace, and joy are some of the fruits of the Spirit.

"A Brother's Gift"

Maureen told me her story during retreat. It was the first time she had shared it. I asked if I could use it for this book, and she smiled broadly and said yes. After a less than successful attempt to write it, I invited her to put it into words herself. She smiled appreciatively and "A Brother's Gift" came in the mail shortly after.

> Weddings are usually happy times of celebrating and rejoicing. Tears of joy mixed with feelings of sadness and hope are to be expected. At my niece's wedding I, too, had mixed feelings: joy for her and hate for her mother.
>
> My niece, the only daughter of my brother, Neil, was to be married two months after his death. As I sat in church waiting for the wedding to begin, I remembered with bitterness the misery my brother

had endured for some years before his death. His wife had seemed to have a need to belittle and demean him even in public. We learned later that she had also been repeatedly unfaithful to him before their divorce.

Neil and I had been not only siblings but also friends. While acknowledging that there are two sides to divorce, he had shared with me his pain at being rejected and humiliated by his wife. I was sure that the unremitting stress had been a contributing factor in his death.

The family members were as one in despising her behavior and had broken off contact with her. They all felt deep resentment, but I felt hate. I was not even willing to try to heal the hate because I believed that to do so would constitute a denial of my brother's pain.

The wedding was just about to begin when my former sister-in-law came up the center aisle with her new husband. Until recently, he had been the husband of one of her friends. They sat just a few seats ahead of me and some family members looked at me to see my reaction. I could not react because I felt rigid and as if I were smothering in a kind of dark bitterness. In the midst of this darkness, I heard my brother's voice. I heard it not with my ears but from deep within me. He said, "Mo, let all of that go. None of it matters anymore."

I find it hard to describe what happened next. I felt as though a heavy, dark blanket had dropped from me and I could breathe deeply. I felt clean and light and peaceful. I looked at the one who had been the object of my hate and felt not only forgiveness but a strong desire to continue to be kind and forgiving.

At the reception following the wedding, I was able to greet and talk in a friendly way with this woman whom I had despised. Family members asked me

> how I could bear to talk to her. I couldn't answer because I was so filled with wonder at the miracle of healing that God had sent me through my brother.
>
> In the years that have followed this experience, I find myself often recalling Neil's words when I am in situations where I need to get back my perspective and restore my inner peace.

Maureen's story is an example of forgiving that comes as gift, as grace. Maureen's brother, now in the Light, was the channel for her to see the light and experience the healing that comes through forgiving. Her story also teaches us that the one who forgives is transformed and his or her actions are different as a result. Joanna North writes, "There is an implicit connection between forgiveness and outward action, for if I forgive someone who is no longer present it is true that if I were to see him again I *would* behave towards him in a different way than if I had not forgiven him."[3] Words and actions reflect the condition of the heart. Maureen's heart was healed, freed from hatred. She was transformed by forgiving.

Passing on the Pain

Some time ago I lived with five other women in a happy and supportive community that consisted of three religious, a volunteer, and two university students. One day Sue, a foreign student, received a phone call saying her father was extremely ill. In the rush to pack and get to the airport, she left without giving us a telephone number or address where we could reach her.

While Sue was en route, we received word that her father had died. That night three of us sat around the table trying to figure out how we could reach her and extend our love, concern, and sympathy. Kimberly pointed to Sue's book bag and said, "Maybe there is an address in there." That innocent comment and our ensuing action would lead us to share in Sue's suffering and pain in a disturbing way.

Kimberly pulled Sue's billfold out of the bag and opened it, looking for some identification with a home address. As she pulled out a stack of bills she remarked, "There is a lot of money here."

I saw a one-hundred dollar bill and had the impression of several more crisp bills. We decided to put the billfold away.

The next day Kathy, Sue's sponsor, called. Kathy had encouraged Sue to live with us so that she could attend classes at the university and learn English. Kathy asked what time she could come to the house to pick up Sue's things. I mentioned that Sue had left behind a big suitcase, some clothes, books, a book bag, and a billfold with a lot of money.

Kathy arrived Thursday afternoon, and I helped her pack up Sue's belongings. Not more than an hour after she left the house, she called me. Sounding tense, she said that Sue had told her there were five or six hundred dollars in the billfold. Kathy said, "Remember, you told me several hundred dollars when we talked on the phone." She sounded extremely upset.

I said, "I don't remember saying several hundred. How much is in the billfold?"

She said, "About two hundred dollars."

I felt that Kathy was accusing me of stealing Sue's money. I got defensive and repeated, "I never said several hundred. And no one in this house would ever take anything."

We each repeated our statements, record-like, several times. Finally, Kathy said, "Well, I have nothing else to say." She hung up.

This phone call took place just before supper. Four of us were home that evening, and we spent the mealtime trying to comprehend what had happened. I left what was meant to be a delicious, delightful meal with a feeling heavy as lead in the pit of my stomach. My mind raced through possibilities like a computer's menu options. The others tried to make me laugh, but I could not let it go. I felt accused.

Dorothy got home late that night. She had been out of town for several days. She remembered Kimberly saying there was a lot of money in the billfold, hundreds of dollars. With that, I felt that Kathy may have been right. Perhaps I did say "several hundred" during our phone conversation. And at that point, I accused Kimberly in my heart.

After a restless night I awoke with a visual image of crisp bills. I decided I wanted to talk with Kimberly. Jeri, Dorothy, and I called her out of bed and reviewed with her all possible scenarios. She said, "What I saw was one hundred and four twenties." That was near the amount Kathy had found. But it did not match what Sue had said to Kathy or what Kathy thought she had heard me say.

We agreed that I would call Kathy again to find out if the twenties were "crisp." Seeing one hundred-dollar bill and some more crisp bills was my only definite memory.

I called Kathy and said I would bring over Sue's tuition refund, which was due in the next day's mail. I wanted her to show me the billfold. Kimberly and I then talked for over an hour. She said, "I believe you all did not take any money. I know I did not." I no longer thought that Kimberly could have taken the money. I thought about the fact that we all loved Sue, but Kimberly had taken her under her wing and had been especially good to her. She had, in fact, offered to put Sue's airline ticket on her own credit card.

Could someone have taken the hundreds and replaced them with twenties? Had I in fact said "several hundred" assuming that the crisp bills I had seen were also hundred-dollar bills, like the one on top? Perhaps they had been twenties all along. I was not sure.

I left Kimberly feeling as accused as I had felt the night before. I spent the rest of the day grappling for alternatives, even scan-

ning my mind for friends and relatives who had been to the house during the critical time period.

The refund check came in the mail, and I took it to my room to put it in my purse. I noticed the envelope was not sealed. Out of fear that Kathy would think I had opened it, I quickly licked it shut. Then I panicked, wondering if the check was still inside. I was becoming paranoid!

I drove to Kathy's house. As I handed her the envelope, I said, "Will you see if it is all right?"

She opened the envelope. No check fell out. My heart dropped. Then she said, "It looks fine." The check was attached to the receipt form, thank God.

I asked Kathy to show me the billfold and to pull out the bills as Kimberly had done several nights before. A one-hundred-dollar bill was on top; there were several crisp twenty dollar bills under it. I said, "This looks exactly like what I saw that night. I didn't realize those were only twenties behind the hundred." I now felt sure that no one had taken any money and that what Kimberly said she saw in the billfold was precisely what was found there.

Kathy apologized for accusing us. We talked over a cup of tea and agreed that she would call Sue. There was still a mystery, but we understood that much can get lost in translation and in panic, and there might be a logical explanation. It was as Jeri had said all along, "What we have here is not a theft but a terrible mistake."

I returned home to tell the others of my newfound conviction that nothing had been taken. (As it turned out, three crisp hundred dollar bills were later found in the inside pocket of Sue's winter coat. Kathy sent us a letter of apology.) Kimberly was telling the truth. We were all relieved. The next morning I approached Kimberly and asked her forgiveness for sparking feelings of mistrust. I felt that I had passed on to her the accusation hurled at me. I created pain for her out of my own pain. How could I do such a thing? Why would I do such a thing?

I came to believe that the answer to my questions was deeply rooted in my family experience. Exploring the family system helped clarify my overreaction, my fear, and my deep pain at being accused.

According to family tales, the paternal side of my family has a propensity for stealing. More serious is an accompanying tendency to disengage from the wrongdoer. Thus, parts of my family have been "cut off" because of suspicion. There are aunts, uncles, and cousins I have never met because of accusations of stealing or cheating that happened before I was born. To have distrust surface caused great anxiety for me. It tapped into my unconscious grief and loss.

William Worden reminds us, "One important reason for looking at a family systems approach is that unresolved grief may not only serve as a key factor in family pathology but may contribute to pathological relationships across the generations."[4] Incomplete mourning, unresolved hurt, unhealed wounds, and unforgiven injury cry out for completion and resolution. A family's unresolved issues surface whenever the opportunity arises: through experiencing similar circumstances, when allowing ourselves to be still, or because of the compassion we feel in the face of another's pain. Each time issues surface or family secrets are brought out in the open, they provide us with the opportunity to see, remember, heal, and integrate them.

To realize that I, too, am capable of the same behavior that I deplored in my family is a humbling experience. Finding myself able to pass on pain led me not to compassion, nor to discovering forgiveness because I'm as culpable as the next person, but to blaming. I blamed my family, which I perceive to be the source of my tendency to mistrust. I did not like finding out that I, too, am the owner of a suspicious nature. The Whiteheads speak to this topic in their book on adult development:

> If forgiveness is hard to give, it is difficult to receive as well. To accept your forgiveness, I, too, must revisit the hurt. I must remember what I did and recall the ways in which you were hurt by it. I will have to acknowledge that I was responsible; I may even have to admit that I was wrong. Here again, I may find it easier to deny all this. It is humbling to need to be forgiven. As long as I am in the right, I have no such need. To accept your forgiveness is to confess my guilt—not only to myself but to you as well.[5]

To acknowledge the need to be forgiven in no way minimizes hurt or wrong done against us. Forgiving and being forgiven are two sides of the same coin. They are related but different. Both are essential for healthy life.

Genogram: A Tree of Life, a Tool for Forgiving

The genogram is an attempt to look back at the family story, understand the movements of the present generation, and spring to the next with hope. It is usually a three-generational map. It shows where we come from, where we are, and where we hope to go as a system, a living organism. Augustus Napier maintains, "The family members move in precise planetary orbits around one another. They are a world, a solar system, a small universe of experience."[6] The family genogram testifies to the fact that not only are we related but whether dead or alive, geographically near or far, psychologically close or distant, we are connected. We influence and are influenced by one another. The genogram is a tool for exploring the nature of these connections and for seeing where ties need to be realigned for the health and development of the whole. Dorothy and Raphael Becvar state, "The genogram provides a visual mapping that may help family members see patterns and relationships in a new light."[7] By using the genogram, we come to see the past from a new angle. This family map provides a context for the emotional experiences of the present. It allows us to take a peek into a healthier, more hopeful future. Working with a genogram helps us see not only the flaws but the gifts each family member brings to the whole.

Family practitioners should create a genogram of their own family system before they engage in counseling others. I also advocate creation of a family genogram by persons in the pastoral care field. It is extremely helpful for anyone wanting or needing to forgive an injurer who is a family member. Initially, working with the genogram may evoke anger. Often, as the visual image of the family story takes shape, this anger is replaced with awe. Finally, we come away from the process with gratitude and understanding that may lead to compassion. Compassion is the spark that ignites our choice to forgive.

In creating your genogram, you will see an image developing and recall long-forgotten stories of both your nuclear and your extended family. Begin with yourself and work backward, sideways, and forward. In the center of the page draw a circle for yourself, if you are female, or a square if you are male. Add your siblings. Draw a horizontal line above yourself and your siblings. At one end of this line draw a circle for your mother; draw a square at the other end for your father. Next, draw a vertical line upward from each parent so you can create each of their family systems. Go back as far as you can. Now you are ready to work with your parents and their siblings, your aunts and uncles. When they are in place, draw a vertical line and place a square or circle for each of their children, your cousins.

Work the same way below the horizontal line with your family and the families of your siblings. Place an X in circles or squares of those who have died. Use connecting lines to show marriages and a double solidus (\\) through a line to indicate a divorce. Number each circle and square and date major events. On a separate paper recount stories you know or have heard about the person associated with each numbered symbol.

Memories will surface as you begin writing, drawing, connecting and disconnecting, and changing relationships. Create your own or new symbols. This is your tree of life. It will be your key to new life, your tool for forgiving.

Begin with a key, an explanation of your symbols. Set the stage with a cursory recounting of events that have had a major influence on the family system. Details will follow as you create the genogram. For example, in the genogram of my family (see page 82), M stands for the maternal branch of the family. The family on the paternal side is marked *P*. My mother is M, and *P* is my father. All of their ancestors and siblings live in Holland and speak only Dutch. *P* and M have three children, ten grandchildren and five great-grandchildren. This part of the family lives in Minnesota. *P* and M and their children are bilingual and have created their own mixture of languages that the grandchildren can somewhat understand. This is a source of both intimacy and of alienation.

The genogram depicts patterns that exist in families. According to Kelly, "These patterns develop as a consequence of the tension generated by attempts to balance the forces of togetherness and individuality."[8] In my family, this tension is significantly complicated by dual languages and cultures, which influence interaction, perspective, communication, humor, and values. The fact that our extended family is separated from us by the Atlantic creates potential enmeshment within the immediate family. Creating a "hybrid language," for example, can foster a kind of privacy that excludes American-born relatives.

As I did my family genogram and came to my place in the system, I saw a small, disconnected circle in the middle of the paper, isolated and lonely. This is not my reality. Though I have no husband or children, I am a member of a large community that shares life, ministry, and a committed future. Thus I encircled myself with many circles and called my symbol a "communogram." This symbol rings true to me. As with any tool, the genogram is meant to assist us in coping with reality, and, as a tool, it is limited. Anyone not following the norm, not presenting the usual patterns within which the tool functions, needs to adapt and adjust the tool, as I did. Many stories of pain, courage, struggle, success, and life-giving creativity—and perhaps a few skeletons in the closet—lie at the root of a genogram/communogram. It is a tree of life.

INTEGRATING THE FINDINGS

It is essential to dig down to the root of pain so we can heal from the inside out. It is important to bring family secrets into the open, keeping in mind the good of the whole as well as the needs of the individual. However, there comes a time to let go of the pain and transcend it. This does not mean to ignore or to suppress our pain, but to go through it and move beyond our anguish. Only then can we receive its teaching and find a new way of being in the world.

This kind of development means accepting a new self definition, a new identity. That, in itself, is a fearful proposition. Sometimes we are attached to our pain. But unless our lives are continually re-created, we get stuck in a quagmire of self-pity and our spiritual lives deaden. Forgiving is a way to clean out the roots, rebuild the structure, and function anew. Non-forgiving adds unnecessary strain to our lives and piles up the healing work for the next generation. Ernest Kurtz and Katherine Ketcham describe resentment as the poison of the spiritual life: "Resentment goes over and over an old injury: revisiting the hurt, the powerlessness, the rage, the fear, the feeling of being wronged. Scraping the scab off the wound, resentment relishes anew its pain; it is the particular kind of memory that reinforces the vision of *self-as-victim*.[9]

Mary Ellen's story taught us that there is hope, resolution, and a peace-filled conclusion to life's struggles and questions. Maureen's experience assured us that forgiveness does happen and that we are guided in the process. Forgiving transforms the wounded one into a healer for others.

Shortly after the episode involving Sue's money, my mother asked me to take care of some family financial affairs. I would not do so without letting everyone involved know the nature of the transactions. My parents wondered why I had this need to explain my actions. I told them the story of how I had passed on the pain. The compassion in my father's eyes gave me great hope. He recognized the source of my pain. The concern in my father's eyes released me of guilt and enabled me to let go of the resentment I carried toward his side of the family. As Joan Boryshenko says, "Our problems, mistakes, sufferings, and regrets have been no less a part of our innate movement toward wholeness than have our conscious efforts to live a life of compassion and love."[10]

The peace with which Mary Ellen died, the radiance on Maureen's face as she told about her ability to forgive, and the release of resentment I experienced in the face of my father's compassion all testify to the fact that forgiving heals. Forgiving frees us from needless anxiety and restores us to the truth of ourselves as good. Jesus taught us this message long ago. It is a story we tend to forget. People like Mary Ellen and Maureen help us to remember it.

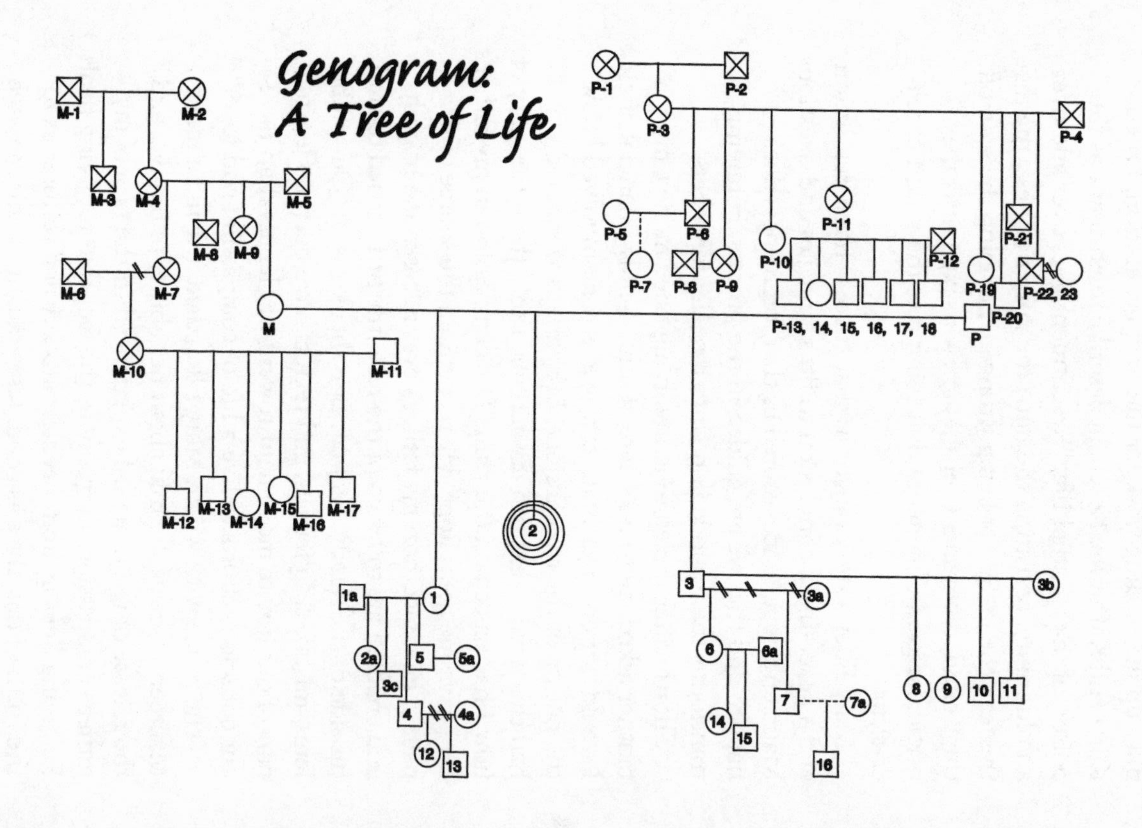

Genogram:
A Tree of Life
M-1
M-2
M-3
M-4
M-5
M-6
M-7
M-8
M-9
M
M-10
M-11
M-12
M-13
M-14
M-15
M-16
M-17
P-1
P-2
P-3
P-4
P-5
P-6
P-7
P-8
P-9
P-10
P-11
P-12
P-13, 14, 15, 16, 17, 18
P-19
P-20
P-21
P-22, 23
P
1
1a
2
2a
3
3a
3b
3c
4
4a
5
5a
6
6a
7
7a
8
9
10
11
12
13
14
15
16

5

Forgiving Systemic Injury

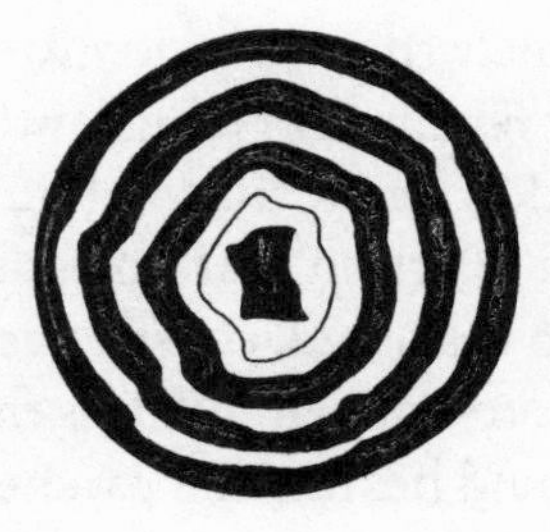

Systems and institutions can hurt, wound, or negatively affect individuals. Forgiveness is essential for healing any injuries. What are the principles of interpersonal forgiveness? Are these principles transferable to systemic injury? In the pages that follow systemic injury is the common denominator for the experiences of a grieving wife, a couple in rural America, and a survivor of the Holocaust. Then we turn to the particular situation of women religious in the Catholic church, who are surviving and flourishing in what many consider to be an oppressive system. A key element in "flourishing" under or after oppression is a forgiving spirit. Oppression promotes either struggle or disengagement. The forgiving spirit produces personal freedom and a tenacious struggle for justice.

Before examining systemic injury, it is important to review some of the multifaceted aspects of forgiving. Forgiving is a choice, an act of the will, a human power. It is learned, and it is a gift of grace. Forgiveness is healing, and necessary for human growth and development. Non-forgiving keeps us trapped and relationally stagnant. Forgiving restores our hope in the future. Relationships may not be reconciled, but through forgiving, we are no longer defined by the pain of the past. A relationship exists, a serious injury occurs, we recognize the wounding as serious, and we set about healing the emotional damage while choosing to forgive. R. S. Downie writes: "The forgiver is required to prevent any barrier remaining permanently between him and the forgivee . . . and to renew trust in him. It is the exhibition of this attitude in action that, together with a belief that injury has been sustained, constitutes forgiveness."[1] Forgiveness releases resentment. This is the first step toward resolving old hurts and healing the psyche.

The family, as our primary system, is the entree into the issue of forgiving systemic injury. Family is our first context for life, nourishment, and growth. It can also be the arena in which we first experience pain, neglect, and abuse that are passed on to us from the past. In families where there is no resolution of traumatic events, "they persist to haunt future generations like a ghost—the proverbial family skeleton."[2] Once forgiving has occurred, the family system is no longer the same.

Communities in which adults are bound by a common vision and shared values are also "families." For such families, mission is an added dimension. It is their reason for being and the motivating force for their caring for and support of one another. Whether we are families tied by blood or communities bound together by a vision, we are one living, breathing organism. The well-being of one member affects the health of the whole. Communities, as well as families, are healthy or dysfunctional, open or closed systems. Both grieve well or with great distress, learn how to forgive, or pass on the pain. Thinking of families and communities as systems impels us to explore institutional injury. It leads us to ask if the principles of interpersonal forgiveness are transferable to systemic injury.

In this chapter we consider persons who most assuredly have been wounded. But their injury is the fault of a system rather than an individual. If the wounded person is able to forgive, the system remains, but it is altered because the injured person is no longer its victim. Forgiving liberates the injured. And because they are interconnected, forgiving benefits the injurers, whether they know it or not, whether they seek forgiveness or not. We experience the consequences of forgiving and non-forgiving on personal, interpersonal, systemic, and cosmic levels. Forgiving adds to the level of goodness in the universe. Resentment, as justified as it might be, lessens the quantity of goodness in the world. Forgiving is the key to the transformation of oppressive social, cultural, and religious systems. Forgiving brings peace to mind and heart and instills in us hope for the world.

Principles of Interpersonal Forgiveness

Seven elements of interpersonal forgiveness have crystallized in this work. I would like to invite readers to reflect on them and on what they see as the underlying principles of interpersonal forgiveness.

First, there exists a relationship based on trust. In the beginning God created the universe out of primordial chaos and saw that it was good. Relationships begin in trust and address our human desire for the good. Interpersonal forgiveness focuses on relationships that have been injured. Trust is betrayed. Hearts are broken. What is good has been damaged.

Second, the injury is named and acknowledged by the victim as serious. It is important for the victim to believe he or she has been wounded. The relationship has been damaged and life will never be the same again. After acknowledging the wound, we can choose how to live with it.

So, preconditions for forgiving are the existence of a good relationship, and injury to that relationship. Acknowledging the hurt involves seeing that not only the relationship but our very sense of self has been seriously damaged. As a result, we experience moral outrage. We demand justice. Claiming the pain requires that we feel it, absorb it, are immersed in it. Only then can the pain empower change. Going through the pain is like the astronauts of Apollo XIII catapulting around the moon; although their path led them further from home, they followed it in order to gain enough energy for the return voyage.

Third, forgiving is initially an act of volition. It is a matter of will. Forgiving is a learned skill, a courageous act that sets us on a long journey of emotional and spiritual healing. The decision to forgive entails release of resentment, to which we have a perfect right in light of the serious injury. It is a choice to forego the desire for revenge, whether blatant or subtle and insidious. Revenge can be as simple as retelling the story of our pain too often or inappropriately. It takes greatness of soul to curb that passion and learn the art of forgiving. The decision to forgive is an act of courage marked by a definite change in action and behavior. Downie reminds us: "In many cases it is easier to play down the extent of the injury and ignore the nature of the moral offense, and so to condone, than it is to face up to the injury and make the effort to forgive."[3] Forgiving is a sign of magnanimity of soul. It is an indication of compassion. It is the mark of a true lover of peace and justice.

Fourth, forgiving is unconditional. This is where forgiving becomes radical, especially in a culture like ours, where law embodies volumes of ramifications for violations and infractions. True forgiving requires nothing of the other—not even remorse or repentance. Oftentimes we confuse forgiveness with reconciliation. The latter is a mutual act reuniting parties who have been separated because of injury. Forgiving, on the other hand, is a solitary act of the will. It is a movement within our own heart. In forgiving, we release resentment, let go of our identity as victim, and forego a feeling of moral superiority over our abuser. Forgiving leads to compassion; it is undertaken out of sincere respect, *agape*, for the personhood of the offender. John Hebl and Robert Enright maintain that unconditional love is the core of forgiveness. They point out that the "one who forgives has suffered a deep hurt, usually revealing an underlying resentment; the offended person has a moral right to resentment, but overcomes it nonetheless; a new response to the other accrues, including compassion and love; this loving response occurs despite the realization that there is no *obligation* to love the offender."[4]

Fifth, there is a moment of grace when one realizes forgiveness has taken place. The choice to forgive sets us on a long and arduous journey through anger, rage, fear, depression, and, sometimes, shame. Finally, we arrive at acceptance of our emotional scars and learn to live well, with our woundedness. Each journey has its own dynamic, its own timing, its side roads and rest stops. But we do reach home; we come home to a peace-filled self. Eventually, we realize that the pain is no longer as intense, the desire for revenge no longer so burning. There is a moment of grace in the forgiving process when the choice to forgive bears fruit, freedom comes, and compassion replaces resentment.

Sixth, forgiving is a healing power. We have the power to forgive or to retain the sins of others as burden on our hearts and in our lives. Forgiving offers us freedom from the burden of resentment so that we, like the stooped woman in the gospel (Lk 13:10–17), no longer have to go through life looking and feeling "down." Because of the healing touch of Jesus, we can go through life with our shoulders up, viewing others eye-to-eye. This is the effect of forgiving, but it is also the effect of being forgiven. Donald Senior and Carroll Stuhlmueller say that in forgiveness, Jesus "'releases' those bound with physical burdens of pain and illness, which the biblical mind recognized as part of the legacy of sin. The case of the woman bent double . . . is typical of this liberating dimension of forgiveness."[5]

Jesus is the teacher of radical forgiveness. He took the initiative, forgave unconditionally, and preserved the worth of the offender. As followers of Jesus, we are called to learn the lessons of forgiving. The choice to forgive is healing because it bestows freedom. In the choice to forgive lies our option for life. Forgiving is done out of compassion and unconditional regard for the wrongdoer. Doris Donnelly says that, in the end, "All forgivers do as Jesus did: they restore self-worth to the offender; they cancel a debt; they confer freedom; and they love beyond their imagining."[6]

Seventh, transformation is the result of forgiving. Forgiving is a change agent because of its healing power for the victim, for the wrongdoer, and for all those affected by the injury. Senior and Stuhlmueller remind us that "Jesus' healing activity demonstrated that the saving grace of God extends not only to personal guilt and broken relationships but to human bodies, to societal structures, to mysterious forces that hold creation itself in check."[7] Forgiving is transforming. It changes our perceptions and alters our desires and life's direction. It results in a new vision of self and renewed activity on behalf of the community. In other words, forgiving initiates a shift of focus, a transformation of reality, for all those affected by the injury.

In summary, forgiveness is our participation in God's life and unconditional love. Forgiving is an action, a choice we make. By this choice we further God's life among us. Forgiving is a private act of will that becomes public in its effects. The power to forgive is ours to use. It is a gift of grace. Forgiving is a teaching of Jesus given so that we can have life and have it to the full. There is healing in forgiving—for the wounded one, for the perpetrator, and for the world as an organic, living system.

What Is a System? How Does It Work?

Words such as *wholeness*, *circle*, *open*, *living*, *organism*, *convergence*, *interwoven*, *cooperative*, *growth*, *hierarchy*, and *control* are frequently associated with systems theory. Each has a raft of meanings and connotations, but common to all is the fact that the system is self-regulating through a process of degeneration and regeneration. In other words, a system has a life/death/resurrection cycle. It is made up of interchangeable parts, and it functions as a whole, an entity unto itself. However, in our culture, we do not tend to look at things systemically. We value individualism and suffer from the delusion of thinking we can control our lives and our planet.

Larry Graham describes a different paradigm for thinking systemically:

> A systemic perspective emphasizes togetherness; our way of life emphasizes separateness. Systemic refers to

> ongoing processes and transactions; we emphasize causes, effects, and outcomes. A systemic orientation affirms both/and; we assume life requires choices between either/or alternatives. A systemic view emphasizes cooperation and reciprocal influence; our way of life emphasizes competition and coercive influence. A systemic view affirms that creative advances include what has gone before; our way of life is built upon the negation of earlier values. Systems analysis underscores the individual's ongoing relationship to society, culture, and nature; our way of thinking underscores the individual's opposition to society, culture, and nature. Systems thought concerns itself with holism; our way of thinking focuses upon the autonomy of the parts in themselves.[8]

Edwin Friedman amplifies the systems theory by adapting it to family and church. The family or community is an organic whole with all parts giving and receiving life from one another. The quality of that exchange determines the health of the system. Friedman points out that systems

> focus less on content and more on the *process* that governs the data; less on the cause-and-effect connections that link bits of information and more on the principles of organization that give data meaning. . . . Each component, therefore, rather than having its own discrete identity or input, operates as a part of a larger whole. *The components do not function according to their "nature" but according to their position in the network.*[9]

In systems thinking we are aware that we are related and that our very presence brings harmony, anxiety, intensity, or healing to the family or community.

Ludwig von Bertalanffy says the open system, "maintains itself in a continuous inflow and outflow, a building up and breaking down of components,"[10] and thus attains a time-independent "steady state," distinct from equilibrium. He warns, "The more parts are specialized in a certain way, the more they are irreplaceable, and loss of parts may lead to the breakdown of the total system."[11] Transformation of the individual alters the system. We know this from our families. The addition of a new baby, the moving out of a young adult, or the death of a family member alters that system irrevocably. Von Bertalanffy maintains, "In the steady state, the composition of the system remains constant in spite of continuous exchange of components."[12] This does not bode well for anyone attempting to alter a system by mere presence or absence. It says the whole is greater than the sum of its parts.

Von Bertalanffy also praises science for approaching systems not as a conglomeration of parts but as organic, living, open, and interactive. Herein lies our hope for transformation! Each part affects the others and the whole by its very being or nonbeing. The system may remain, but its quality and impact are affected by its members' relationships with one another. Parts of a system may be interchangeable and persons seem dispensable, but the good news of the Christian life includes the truth that we are good, that we are unique and irreplaceable. All things are related. We are bonded consciously or unconsciously because of our very existence in this universe. One life influences all creation by its being or nonbeing on this limited planet.

Identifying Systemic Injury

We have only to remember our violent history, to read the newspapers of today, to watch television, or to listen to the people in our families and our communities to realize that we are immersed in social injustice. Systemic injury is the hurt felt by an individual as the result of the unjust actions of a group, a society, a system, or an institution. Examples of systemic injury include a government that aims to "reform" the welfare system at the expense of the poor, blaming the poor for their poverty rather than looking at ways our economic system inherently creates poverty; women who endure the judgment of a health-care system that funds more studies for men, thereby minimizing women's health issues; power differences in church and family that keep women economically dependent and vulnerable to abuse or battering. Maxine Glaz and Jeanne Moessner have edited a book that explores gender-specific assumptions that underlie even the field of pastoral care. They remind us that "sexism creates unnecessary problems for women's development and undue constrictions of the feminine personality. Moreover, these constrictions are social, systemic, and external to the individual woman."[13]

The following three stories all deal with systemic injury. The first two show the importance of recognizing the wound. The third moves beyond recognition to forgiveness.

A Wife's Grief

Systemic injury is recounted in the grief of a mother whose son's untimely death was preventable, and in the struggle for justice on the part of the son's wife, whom I shall call Eileen.

Eileen is a young mother of three children. Her husband was the foreman of a plant that had been using toxic chemicals for several weeks. He sat at his desk, breathing the fumes day in and day out. One night at home, his breathing became extraordinarily heavy. Eileen could not wake him and called for emergency help.

Paramedics could not get a tube down his throat; his esophagus was swollen and blocked. He died two hours later. The diagnosis was heart failure.

Eileen brought the case to court, amidst her own grieving and trying to raise her children. She fought the "system" for the truth and in the hope of receiving worker's compensation. Several doctors claimed her husband died of heart failure. But another said the fumes could have caused the difficulty in breathing that, in turn, caused the heart failure. The court ruled in favor of the company.

Women and children struggling for survival are primary victims of systemic injury.

Ann and Jack

In our culture the rural family is often idealized. A farm is a great place to raise children. Life is respected, the earth is reverenced, and the family is valued. Yet here too insidious and not-so-subtle patriarchy keeps the farm wife "in her place."

Ann and her husband, Jack, cashed in their life savings and bought cows. They struggled for five years trying to make their small dairy farm viable. For a variety of reasons, they were finally forced to cash in their chips, auction their small herd of dairy cattle, and abandon their dream.

Ann tells of the frustration of assigned male/female roles supported by both men and women. For example, some bankers would talk only to "the man of the house," though she was the one who had run the business aspects of the farm. As a woman, her opinion was neither sought nor valued. If her opinion was given, she was ignored. Devaluation, negation, and dismissal are often the lot of women who speak up or who want to function outside defined boundaries in a patriarchal system.

Is it any wonder that the consequence of such diminishment and wounding to self-esteem is anger? Jack, too, was frustrated with unnecessary limitations placed on his wife—and therefore on their family business and harmony—by patriarchy. "They can't even see it. They are oblivious. It takes an outsider to see it," he said. Both women and men are negatively affected by patriarchy.

A Survivor's Story

Nathan is a Polish Jew and a survivor of Nazi concentration camps. He was selected at age fourteen for the camps; his little brother was killed. To this day he does not know what happened to his mother. He declares that he bears no hatred toward his oppressors. He himself does not fully understand how or why this can be. The ability to forgive is a mystery to him. We might call it a grace. It is even more of a mystery, since Nathan claims he is personally prone to holding grudges and is very sensitive to slights or mistreatment.

Nathan has learned that it is often easier to forgive an enemy than one's own people for an injury. It had surprised him to find that returning to Germany in 1965 was easier than returning to his native Poland. The maltreatment he received at the hands of his own people had done much more damage. The others were "enemies," but the Polish people were his own. Between the years 1939 and 1945, Jews were treated as subhuman. Being forced, as a Jew, to live in an ever-diminishing ghetto carried with it the pain of a family feud or civil war. Even before the war, anti-Semitism was very strong, and the pain was intensified.

Nathan also points out that those who suffer more directly seem to have less hatred than those who suffer indirectly. Could it be that members of the generation suffering directly are more ready to forgive because they have been confronted with issues of immediate survival?

Von Bertalanffy reports a view similar to Nathan's after studies done with World War II survivors:

> The behavioristic experiment led to results contrary to expectation. World War II—a period of extreme physiological and psychological—stress did not produce an increase in neurotic (Opler, 1956) or psychotic (Llavero,1957) disorders, apart from direct shock effects such as combat neuroses. In contrast, the affluent society produced an unprecedented number of mentally ill. Precisely under conditions of reduction of tensions and gratification of biological needs, novel forms of mental disorder appeared as existential neurosis, malignant boredom, and retirement neurosis (Alexander, 1960), i.e., forms of mental dysfunction originating not from repressed drives, from unfulfilled needs, or from stress but from the meaninglessness of life.[14]

Could it be that those who suffered most directly forgive more easily because they have seen the face of the oppressor? Seeing our enemy allows us to reach out in compassion. Etty Hillesum prayed for the sullen, disgruntled, and, from her perspective, weak Gestapo officer who led her to the death camp.

In systemic thinking, what injures one wounds us all. The survival instinct carries us through the initial state of shock. Later reflection upon the injury and the nature of the relationship determines the difficulty of our choice to forgive. Awareness that we too have been wounded when there is injury to our loved ones allows us to expand the definition of interpersonal forgiving. We come to realize that even though we may not have been injured directly, we too have the need to forgive. Family systems have taught us that wounding of one generation may require another form of forgiving from the next generation. Carl Bråkenhielm supports this view by pointing out that "the right to forgive is not exclusively tied to the person who has suffered a direct injustice. Another person who is able to identify in a unique sense with the injured party can in effect become party to the right to forgive. This ability to identify is as a rule greater among persons who are closely related."[15]

Nathan's is a story of mysterious grace. He embodies a free and forgiving heart. His life seems to support the theory that forgiveness happens, that forgiveness is discovered. Remember John Patton's comment from chapter 1—"I am more like those who have hurt me than different from them."[16] According to the discovery of forgiveness theory, we realize that in similar circumstances we might do likewise. That awareness leads us to forgive. Nathan told students who asked him what the Gestapo were like that "without the uniform they looked like you and me."[17] In other words, "There, but for the grace of God, go I."

WOMEN IN THE CATHOLIC CHURCH

Women have a real problem in our sexist church and culture. Women share a history of oppression with more than half the world's population. Ecclesial women have been unduly regulated by patriarchal systems. Yet women religious have had a history of access to power and decision-making that was, until recent times, unavailable to other American women. With the gift of their lives, sisters built the second largest school system in the world, established a growing health-care system, created social networks to help the poor, and ministered where others would not go. Sisters have a proud history in spite of their marginality.

The Gift of Women Religious

Women religious have much to offer society, despite crises of aging and diminishing numbers. They model various forms of common life in a culture that has lost a sense of connection. Women religious show that it is possible to move in and out of leadership roles, with grace and style, in a society where leadership and political issues and "mud-slinging" are synonymous. Patricia Wittberg writes, "Women religious have had experiences that other women have only recently begun to acquire in centuries-old networks and mentoring systems, in ideals of sisterhood, in role modeling of leadership and responsibility, and most recently, in attempts at collaborative, non-hierarchical government."[18]

Ministry to the poor is a primary option in spite of the fact that financial needs in religious communities bring the concept of "national debt" close to home. The orders have many "grandmothers" to care for, and the values that undergird religious life in community are often negated by the culture. Nevertheless, women religious do not exhibit characteristics that mark declining organizations. Conflict, in-fighting, turf battles, unwillingness to risk, and a concentration on personal interests that signal the "death rattle" for organizations are not generally the experience of religious communities. Instead, "women's religious communities are doing the opposite—celebrating, risk-taking, blurring the boundaries of their orders in solidarity with the poor, and committing their resources toward systemic change, not for their own survival, but for the empowerment of the most oppressed. They show a striking deviation from expected behavior."[19]

The Crisis in Women's Religious Communities

Crisis comes in the experience of change that is perceived as loss. It is a turning point, a time of danger as well as opportunity. Crisis is not always a one-time event; it may be a space through which we traverse many times, each time at a deeper level. Developmental crisis reigns in the lives of many communities of women religious today. This crisis covers psychic, historical, geographic, futuristic, and spiritual space. It is like a river that flows through personal identity, ministry, and community. One way to portage crisis, this fast-moving river, is by forgiving.

Each religious community, as an organization, shares characteristics similar to individuals. Normal human developmental stages are initiated by crisis and cover such events as birth, growth, vocation choice, loss, and death. What are the normal developmental crises for an organization? What are the coping skills necessary to live through them well and not merely survive?

Like all of life, coping skills follow a life/death/resurrection pattern. Coping skills for the stresses of necessary transitions need to be flexible, creative, and rooted in prayer. At the crossroad of decision for transformation rather than extinction, religious communities have opted for new life on their terms: freedom, mutuality, and care for the poor. To live into that choice will require healing and forgiving of injuries done by the larger system of which religious communities are a part.

Developmental crises, in human life and human systems alike, are precisely what it means to live. They are natural. The choice as to how well we live is ours. Death for ourselves, our families, or our institutions is but a space on the continuum of life. Each turn of the road presents us with an opportunity for letting go or hanging on to the pain of injury. Each fork in the road allows us to choose to forgive or to go on through life burdened by resentment and anger. "I have set before you life and death, the blessing and the curse. Choose life, then, that you and your descendants may live" (Dt 30:19).

The Hope for Women's Religious Communities

It appears that women religious have made their crisis an occasion and opportunity for growth. They are creatively peering into a new future. Challenging the patriarchal system that oppresses women and letting go of the security and comfort that patriarchal structures provide are accomplished by striving for justice and choosing to forgive. Forgiveness and justice are twins, born of the same mother. Her name is compassion. Grieving well, ritualizing passages, and taking care of our precious selves in the process are ways we support our power to forgive while struggling for justice.

Diarmuid O'Murchu claims that religious life exists and will always need to exist for the sake of the culture, which

> unconsciously rather than consciously . . . sets aside certain individuals and groups and endows them with intensive value systems. It projects onto these liminal groups its deepest hopes, dreams and aspirations and requests the liminal person or group to embody and articulate for society at large the deepest values the society holds sacred.[20]

Recognition of this truth will foster understanding of religious life by a society that is itself in transition from a focus on individualism toward systemic thinking. People long for a community, to be a part of something greater than the individual self. The church is blessed to have members who publicly profess the good of the whole without devaluing the individual. Unequal access to power, however, needs correction. Nonrecognition, shunning, or outright attacks on women's right to exist are matters for forgiving, both in society and in the Catholic church.

Dual Options

Many men and women "lost heart" after Pope John Paul's statement reiterating the ban on women's ordination. The *New York Times*, on page 1 of the May 31, 1994, issue, quoted the pontiff as saying that "the church has no authority whatsoever to confer priestly ordination on women and that this judgment is to be definitively held by all the church's faithful."

In response to this statement, a parishioner I call Fred wrote the following to his bishop:

> This letter is written to announce my resignation from any formal, participating membership in the Roman Catholic Church. . . . The essential crisis in this matter is that my free will has been violated. . . . The social, legal, and psychological restrictions on women—by no means just in the area of ordination—are neither theologically nor scripturally valid and are only a human tradition maintained by men to favor men.

Fred talked with me about his letter to the bishop. He was active member of our Catholic community. He opted for resignation from the church as his mode of protest. My response to him was this: "You will have a great impact in bringing about justice by going. I will, by staying. I need to stay within, to be an irritant to the system, in order to speak my 'peace.' You, on the other hand, being a lay man of influence, have more power to change the system by redirecting your energies. God bless us both."

Carolyn Osiek also maintains that sexism and patriarchy offend both men and women.

> [The first way is to] dehumanize women institutionally and disqualify them on the basis of sex from access to the sacred and to leadership. The second way is to attempt theological justification of the oppression of patriarchalism, so that it would seem to be perpetrated in the name of God. The third way is that sexism works against all of us is by promoting a "false consciousness" which permits both oppressor and oppressed to blindly accept and internalize their roles.[21]

The questions of why to stay in the church and what to do if one remains are two separate but related issues for living within an oppressive system. Nathan's reference to the intensified pain of betrayal by a compatriot underscores why the pain of women in the church is so great. As the topic of conversation turned to women in the church today, Nathan asked how anyone could stay with a system that denigrates its own members. I can understand where his question comes from, given his childhood experiences. It is also the question many women ask themselves. For those who have chosen to remain in the church in spite of its serious limitations, transformation of the oppressive aspects of the institutional church becomes their "call." They remain in the church because they see an overriding value in the sacramental system it offers, a message of hope through the gospel it preaches, a powerful challenge to injustice in its social teachings, and the promise of new life among supportive communities of faith.

There are two approaches to responding to injustice: speak and disengage; or stay and be a "burr under the saddle." We must judge for ourselves which is the most effective action, which approach God is calling us to undertake. Either path motivates and redirects personal energy. Either path moves us out of the victim mentality and causes us to take the initiative. We take overt or covert action. Action is the fruit of contemplation. Whether we choose disengagement and making the reason public or staying in the system to labor for justice, we alter the system. However, either direction is undertaken effectively only after personal freedom and a transformation that is the consequence of having forgiven.

Oppression and wrongdoing exist. Women in the Catholic church are diminished and ignored simply for being women in a male-dominated church. Or they are placed on a pedestal, admired but out of reach. These are two sides of the coin of sexism. Women in the church experience both and are seriously offended by the prejudice inherent in each.

Transfer and Transformation

Transformation is a consequence of the choice to forgive. There are four phases in the forgiving process. First, we discover, claim, and articulate the wrongdoing as injurious. Second, we choose to forgive and let go of rightful resentment. Third, we approach compassion and forgive unconditionally. Finally, by the grace of God, we are transformed. We are free. We see in a new way and relate accordingly. It is the stance itself—our freedom from personal agenda—that has already altered the system. As a result of forgiving, we no longer act out of revenge or righteousness, but with the same power and love that inflamed the hearts of the prophets of old and energized them to speak on behalf of the poor and oppressed.

The principles of interpersonal forgiveness are transferrable to systemic injury. Those injured by systemic injustice have a significant relationship to the system. They are integral members of the whole. As a part of the system's organic life, they have sustained serious injury, know it, speak out against it, ask questions about the way things are, and attempt to find allies and companions on the journey toward a new creation. It is important that there be a sizable component of the system committed to one another and to change. But, for each and all on the journey, forgiving will be the primary and major step; it is the conscious choice for love, in the face of sin. While we make absolutely no demands for change, the very fact that we choose to forgive brings about transformation—in ourselves and, thus, in the system.

The moment of grace in forgiving systemic injury is often letting go of the desire for revenge. Osiek speaks about the call to conversion that is, first of all, forgiveness of those who have wronged us. She writes, "Conversion requires that women forgo the pleasure of hurting back for all the hurt they and their foremothers have received. It requires that power not be misused for still more destructive purposes."[22]

Forgiving systemic injury has healing, transformative power. It is rooted in the premise that love has greater power than hatred. We may set out to alter the system, to bring about justice, but even justice is not a prerequisite for forgiving. Forgiving is unconditional. Unconditional forgiveness, as love, is a paradox. And it is our call. A lover of the church, for example, sees the reality yet sustains hope. She feels her pain and joy intensely, and she confronts the church with the truth of its wounding. Ultimately she forgives with full knowledge and great courage. And thus the system is transformed and the world is renewed.

See, I am doing something new!
Now it springs forth, do you not perceive it?
—Isaiah 43:19

CONCLUSION

Transformation occurs in those healed, who become healers of the very system that inflicted the wounds. A woman in the church, for example, may through the process of forgiving become a preacher for justice, a herald of hope, and thus a healer of the very system that inflicted the injury. The Whiteheads summarize the forgiving process well:

> Forgiving involves a decision, but it is not completed in the moment of choice. Forgiveness is a process, the process of gradually allowing the hurt to heal and rebuilding the experience of trust between us. This process of forgiving does not bring us back to "where we were." It does not allow us "to go on as if nothing has happened." Something *has* happened, something profound. There has been a tear in the fabric of our interwoven lives. Yet we can choose not to be defined by this rupture but instead to incorporate it as part of an ongoing relationship. Our hope is that the hurt we have experienced will not become the pattern, but we sense its contribution of depth and substance to the design.[23]

Forgiving systemic injury causes transformation of the system. A change in one part alters the whole. Change in a system incurs a chain reaction, resulting in a leap of consciousness by the whole organism. This is our hope.

6

The Fourfold Journey of Forgiving

A Road Map for the Way

As you set out on your forgiving journey, I invite you to set aside at least an hour on each of four days, or, better yet, give yourself four full days as healing time. The terms *hour* or *day* are meant symbolically; as with the seven days of creation, they are not to be viewed in a linear manner. Setting aside time is in itself a choice to initiate the possibility of forgiving. If you have already chosen to forgive someone but do not yet experience the freedom of having truly forgiven, this time will encourage you to continue to use your power of forgiving and pray for the grace to have it actually happen.

Giving yourself an entire day for each stop along the journey toward greater healing and wholeness can best be done in an authentic retreat setting. You may join a group in a beautiful environment or sacred place to share silence, scripture, meditation, and the creation of mandalas. Such an environment can also provide for individual conferences with a retreat director or a person willing to serve as a companion on your journey.

The route of the forgiving journey will take you along the four directions of the compass. You begin in the *South*, the place of awakening and breakthrough, where you become aware of the magnitude of the injury. Next, you move to the *West*, the place of suffering and loss, where you experience a darkness that is painful but not evil. Like the womb and the earth itself, this darkness holds the potential for new life and teaches compassion. Then, you move to the *North*, the place of dreams and vision, where you make a clear choice to forgive. Finally, you arrive in the *East*, transformed by wisdom and the ability to accept and see your life, even your injurer, in a new light.

It is important to remember that a person does not make this forgiving journey once and for all. Forgiving takes time and it is a cyclic process. What follows is the description of one way to come to forgive. To each "day" or "hour" I have assigned a portion of the Prologue of John's Gospel, appropriate scripture, prophets, virtues, images, symbols, elements of creation, and a mode of prayer. I have incorporated the square, triangle, cross, and spiral as signs for each direction, incorporating them all within the circle, because these symbols have similar meanings in all cultures and religions.[1] Some aspects of the Native American Medicine Wheel[2] also will help mark the significance of each rest stop on the journey.

Begin in a circle. If you are among others, the group becomes the circle and you create a center in the circle. The center may consist of a bible, a candle, or another symbol that will focus the group. If you are alone, you become the center and create a circle around yourself. The circle is the symbol for eternity, wholeness, unity, and perfection. The circle within the circle, like the pupil in the eye or the wine in the chalice, represents the presence of God. This whole process takes place in the company of God, who journeys with you in joy, pain, sorrow, loss, and grief, as well as in moments of ecstasy and times we reach out to others in compassion and service.

Mandala Creation: A Guide to Self-Reflection

A mandala is a transcultural symbol for the pattern of the universe. It is found in Navaho sand paintings, the rose windows of European cathedrals, in the Aztec calendar, the Hindu "Wheel of Life," and much of natural creation. The mystic Hildegard of Bingen used mandalas to create her images of God and of the universe. Psychologist Carl Jung used them for self-healing and as a tool for bringing order into the chaotic psyches of his clients. Jung reminds us:

> Whereas ritual mandalas always display a definite style and a limited number of typical motifs as their content, individual mandalas make use of a well-nigh unlimited wealth of motifs and symbolic allusions. . . . Images of this kind have under certain circumstances a considerable therapeutic effect on their authors . . . but only when it is done spontaneously. Nothing can be expected from an artificial repetition or a deliberate imitation of such images.[3]

We do not merely look at mandalas. We draw, dream, or dance them. In the circle, we sit in a mandala. Mandalas, like dreams, are a message to us from our subconscious. And, like dreams, they are vehicles through which God speaks to us. We are ultimately transformed by our mandala. When we come to work through issues of forgiveness, routine drawing of mandalas, like journaling, may help us work through the various stages of the process. Like dreams, mandalas can be interpreted only by the one to whom they are given, though others can share their insights into their meaning. Mandala creation as a form of meditation and prayer is in itself healing. It also provides the creator with clues to his or her progress on the journey of forgiving. Mandala creation facilitates awareness of our link with God, for "the mandala, though only a symbol of the self as the psychic totality, is at the same time a God-image, for the central point, circle, and quaternity are well-known symbols for the deity."[4]

As with any form of prayer, there is a method that helps the process. I present here a ten-step "mandala movement" that has allowed many retreatants to experience the inner healing that comes from creating a mandala and meditating with mandalas. (*You will need to read through the steps and gather materials before you actually work through the process.*)

Step one is informational. A mandala basically consists of a circle with a center and four directions. It is important to know the symbolic significance of the circle as eternal, the center as God, and the directions as wholeness. It helps to be familiar with the materials—paper, oil pastels, chalk, watercolors, sand—and their purposes, qualities, and limitations.

Step two is taking time to center. Having the basic framework of a circle, with a center and four directions and finding comfort with tools permit you to let go of your preconceived notions, desired outcomes, or anxiety about the process, your "shoulds." Sit in silence, breathe deeply, relax, and become empty. This step alone may take five to ten minutes.

Step three is a purification ritual. This can be as simple as washing your hands. Washing hands is a literal and symbolic preparation for being in touch with the sacred, with new life. Hand-washing can be combined with a ritual or literal crossing over a threshold into "sacred space," an area where the materials and tables are set up for mandala creation.

Step four is experiencing the void. Stand ready, centered, and purified before a large, blank sheet of paper—and wait. This is a time to trust, invite, and tolerate the impasse that allows the creative act to take place. Being in this state takes great patience and requires letting go of the urge to act and produce.

Step five is containing the chaos. Chaos follows the void. Images surface, colors draw you almost simultaneously, shapes and lines begin to form and bring you to a state of awareness that could be overwhelming without the framework. The circle provides the necessary boundary to contain the chaos. This moment of confusion seems eternal. You survive it only because you have faith that the Spirit will hover over the chaos, as it did over the first chaos, and breathe life into it.

Step six is the actual creation of a mandala. Like all creative movements, mandala creation comes from the inside out. The mandala is the fruit of the breath of the Spirit. Your mandala comes from an energy that is within you, yet greater than you. The mandala is yours, but more than your creation.

Step seven is contemplation. Stand back in awe and gaze at your mandala from all sides, with an admiration that mirrors abandon. This is the essence of the contemplative act. Contemplation is also embracing, with gratitude and love, the message given by God and your true self to your conscious self.

Step eight is transformation. The creative act is in itself transformative. Contemplation enhances and intensifies transformation. When you claim what you see in the mandala, name it, perhaps even write a verse about it, making it your own in whatever way possible, the mandala's message transforms you.

Step nine is reintegration. Take the message of the mandala into your heart and life and allow it to become a source of wisdom. Reintegration of the message means that you take the truth of creation, assimilate it anew, and find nourishment therein. Now your life is lived from the inside out, with renewed vision, energy, hope, and purpose.

Step ten is the destruction of the mandala. The mandala's gift was vision; its physical form need not be retained. It may take some time to let go of the medium of the message. But it is the creation of the mandala and the truth of the mandala, not the mandala itself, that gives you new life. This realization enables you to destroy the mandala by disposing of it—burning it or giving it away. Destruction of the form allows you to reincorporate the energy and truth of the message into your conscious life. This final step is usually done after the completion of the four "hours" or "days." This allows you to see, in concrete images, the flow of your mandala movement and to recall particular insights gained at each stop on your journey.

In the beginning was the Word,
and the Word was with God,
and the Word was God.
—John 1:1

The Beginnings: Discovering the Injury

Beginnings, birth, warmth, and "waking up" to the fact that we are loved by God are some of the characteristics of the *South* (the chart on page 129 summarizes the characteristics for each direction). Its season is *summer*, and its element is *water*. The image is that of the ocean. The waters of the womb, the waters of the unconscious, and the waters of baptism all remind us of our beginnings. *Red* is the color of the South, the color of our life's blood. South's virtue is *respect*, respect for all life. This is a place where we honor ourselves and others. The sign of life is the *square*, the cornerstone that represents stability, security, solidity, responsibility, and completion. This is the pre-injury sense of self. It is the mystical state of *breakthrough*, of feeling loved, of sitting, like Mary, at the feet of Jesus. We find ourselves keenly aware of the presence of God. The angel assigned to the South is the Archangel Gabriel, whose name means "Strength of God."[5] The experience of ourselves as in God and God in us is a strong *emotion*. The prayer of *thanksgiving* is the natural response to this emotion.

Scriptural Reflection

The name given to our God from the beginning is Elohim—energy, power, the strength of God, the Almighty, who journeys *with* us. Elohim, the Almighty, works marvels in us. The Almighty guides us and leads us on our way. The Almighty is personified perfectly in Jesus: the Way, the Truth, and the Life. Elohim knows light and darkness, day and night, goodness and evil. Elohim has the power to bring good out of evil, as the seed must die to bring forth new life. We share the power of the Almighty whenever conflicts are reconciled, whenever we allow God to work good out of evil in and through us.[6] Then we, like Mary, proclaim, "The Mighty One has done great things for me" (Lk 1:49), and we give birth to God in this world. The gospel of the South is *Matthew*, for this book begins with the genealogy of Jesus. It is fitting that *Jeremiah* is the major prophet who journeys with us in our beginnings, for Jeremiah was called before he was born.

> Before I formed you in the womb, I knew you;
> before you were born I dedicated you.
>
> —Jeremiah 1:4

Application to Forgiving

A day of reflection can focus on all kinds of beginnings. Picturing our pre-birth and birth experiences in prayer may be revealing and healing. We pray that God will heal us of our birthing traumas and that we might be rejuvenated in imagining our birthing wonders. We ask that God remove any doubt, fear, or feelings of insecurity that may have come to us in our mother's womb from past generations—free us from needless guilt we may have incurred at causing another suffering because of our coming into this world, and help us, instead, feel for the rest of our lives, in the marrow of our bones, the miracle of life.

We may also take time to explore family roots, peek into closets, and do exercises in which we "step back" into the shoes of our mothers or fathers, grandparents, and great-grandparents, and take on their joys, sorrows, struggles, and wisdom, aiding us in appreciation and compassion. These activities may result in surfacing, facing, and acknowledging serious injury. Just as God's loving presence is felt to be a *breakthrough* of consciousness, after which one is never the same again, so these experiences may lead to a breakthrough of defenses, denial, or events repressed and the accompanying realization that we are permanently wounded and changed. The South is a place of strong emotion. That emotion may be anger. At this time we name the pain and look for its meaning in our lives.

Beverly Flanigan writes: "In a way, forgiving is only for the brave. It is for those people who are willing to confront their pain, accept themselves as permanently changed, and make difficult choices."[7] In understanding just what we are called to forgive, it is necessary to see it, face it, and name it. In so doing, we explore the dimensions of the pain. "In the naming phase, you construct the meaning of the wound. . . . You also identify the meaning of the injury in terms of its duration, controllability, consequences and to some lesser extent, its cause."[8]

The place of beginnings—discovering the injury, naming the pain, and exploring its damage—launches us on the forgiving journey. The place of beginnings is a good place. It provides the foundation for building a new life, as the sign of the square attests. There is pain in the awareness of our injury, but comfort in the realization that we do have guides like the Archangel Gabriel, the "Strength of God," to support us in our genesis. It is a comfort to recall that we have a network of support and nurturing love that has carried us through life thus far, despite our wounding. Beyond the pain and anger we can discern a benevolent power that has protected us and is calling forth from us the great sacrifice of letting go of retaliation.

While in this place, begin drawing your first mandala.
Follow the steps set forth at the beginning of this chapter.

He was in the world,
and the world came to be through him,

but the world did not know him.
He came to what was his own,
but his own people did not accept him.
—John 1:10-11

THE STRUGGLE: APPROACHING COMPASSION

The movement to the *West* is culminated in the experience of letting go, of loss, death, emptiness. Here we come in touch with our center, our true self, through fasting, silence, the solitude of retreats, illness, suffering, and loss. Storms often come from the West, thus the virtue called upon while living in this state is *courage*. It is most fitting that our angelic guide in the West is the Archangel Raphael, whose name means "Healer of God," because despair and the absence of God are frequently experienced in this state. Mystics call it the "dark night of the soul." We come to know the truth of Meister Eckhart's claim that "God is not found in the soul by adding anything but by a process of subtraction."[9] The experience of pain, turmoil, fear, emptiness, and darkness that is part of life in the West is intensified in the feeling that we have lost our "center." But God is always at home with us; it is we who get out of balance and lost. When we come to our senses and return to God, our prayer becomes an expression of *sorrow*. When we have been hurt as a result of the imbalanced choices of another, our prayer can become an expression of sorrow for the one who has hurt us. Our prayer of sorrow is for the pain in our lives and for the damage done to significant relationships. Sorrow here is not the result of pity but the root of true compassion. Being in our own darkness helps us understand another's blindness.

The element of the West is *earth*, its color is *black*, its image is the desert, and its season is *autumn*. This season reminds us of death. Learning to die on many levels teaches us little by little to live without hate and to be without fear. It teaches us to say yes in faith, so that we can freely say the ultimate yes to death itself. The sign I have given to the West is the *cross*, which symbolizes mutuality of relationship, balance, and integration. The cross is the symbol of victory over death. Sleep reminds us of death, and sleep is the most natural regression for us to the comfort of darkness and the security of the womb. Sleep is also the symbol of the inward journey that takes us out of the ego to the true self. That is why Meister Eckhart can rightfully say that "nothing resembles God in all creatures so much as repose."[10] The darkness of this season is associated not only with death but with potential for life; the darkness of the earth is associated with the womb. Life has its beginnings in darkness. To be in the West is to take an introspective journey, one that may be lonely and is often painful. But the West is also is the place of "meetings" for lovers and potential for life.

Scriptural Reflection

The gospel of the West is *Luke*, who is symbolized by the ox, a beast of burden. *Isaiah* is the major prophet of the West. Isaiah describes the role and mission of the Suffering Servant. The Suffering Servant's calling is to proclaim God's favor toward the oppressed, to suffer, and ultimately to be exalted by God. The Suffering Servant, the Messiah, is to establish peace and justice and propagate knowledge of God. He is to be a personal witness to the loving presence of God. As the servant of Yahweh, the Messiah is an individual called by God and filled with the Spirit of Yahweh. He is sent as a teacher of the people, a light to the nations. He is a gentle preacher of the law of God, the love of God. He is despised and rejected, and he purchases our salvation by sacrificing his own life. The servant of Yahweh is ultimately vindicated by God, who sustains him. There are four "servant songs" in Isaiah (Is 42:1-9; 49:1-6; 50:4-11; and 52:13, 53:12). These songs present a mysterious servant, a particular person, who is called by Yahweh while still in his mother's womb:

> The LORD called me from birth,
> from my mother's womb he gave me my name.
> —Isaiah 49:1

The servant was formed by Yahweh, who filled him with the Spirit of Yahweh.

> For now the LORD has spoken
> who formed me as his servant from the womb.
> —Isaiah 49:5

He performs his tasks gently, without display, in a serene manner, and with compassion:

> Not crying out, not shouting,
> not making his voice heard in the street.
> —Isaiah 42:2

He even appears to fail in his task:

> Though I thought I had toiled in vain,
> and for nothing, uselessly, spent my strength,
> Yet my reward is with the LORD,
> my recompense is with my God.
> —Isaiah 49:4

He accepts outrage and contempt:

> And I have not rebelled,
> have not turned back.

I gave my back to those who beat me,
  my cheeks to those who plucked my beard;
My face I did not shield
  from buffets and spitting.

—Isaiah 50:5-6

He does not succumb because Yahweh sustains him:

The Lord GOD is my help,
  therefore I am not disgraced;
I have set my face like flint,
  knowing that I shall not be put to shame.

—Isaiah 50:7

The fourth song, some details of which may have been inspired by the life of the prophet Jeremiah, considers the nature of the suffering of the servant of Yahweh. Like Job, he is innocent yet treated as an evildoer whom God has punished with his suffering. He is condemned to a shameful death. From this atoning suffering, Yahweh, the Almighty, brings salvation to all.

Because of his affliction
  he shall see the light in fullness of days;
Through his suffering, my servant shall justify
    many,
  and their guilt he shall bear.

—Isaiah 53:11

Application to Forgiving

The Suffering Servant and the person letting go of serious injury and forgiving the wrongdoer have much in common. The wounded one is afflicted, sees the light, bears the guilt of many, and finally takes upon himself or herself the pain, lets it die there, not passing it on in any other form. Many who would have suffered are freed. Many are justified. The cycle is broken, and healing can happen. God is with those who suffer. God does not take our suffering away, does not alter it, but joins us in it. God became a man of suffering who laid down his life so that we may have life. God became a man of suffering who could have retaliated and did not. When wronged, in all justice we can demand an apology, retribution, amendment, or a change of heart. If these things come, fine. But our forgiving does not depend on them. Bråkenhielm claims that "forgiveness must be unconditional: only unconditional forgiveness can give expression to that confidence or trust that gives back to the wrongdoer his or her feelings of human worth or dignity."[11] We, like Jesus, can love unconditionally; we have the power to choose compassion. "Let the one among you who is without sin be the first to throw a stone at her" (Jn 8:7).

Draw your mandala. Contemplate its message to you. Share it with a companion or with the group. Then, spend some time during the night being awake and consciously sitting with the darkness. It, too, has a message for you.

The light shines in the darkness,
and the darkness has not overcome it. . . .
The true light, which enlightens everyone,
was coming into the world.
—John 1:5, 9

THE HOPE: CHOOSING TO FORGIVE

Maturity, fullness, purposefulness, vision, and activity are some characteristics of the *North*. The element of the North is *air*. It is the breath of life. *White* is the color of the North, the color of purification and *winter*. The entire earth purifies itself continually, as does the individual, especially during mature years. Spiritually speaking, we purify ourselves of anxiety, doubt, and fear. We learn to walk alone rather than depending upon the nurturing love of God. The virtue is *generosity*, for as we mature, we learn to share our gifts with others. It is natural that the prayer of the north is *petition*, because providing for the well-being of others is the work of this place. Concern for others is the life task of this state. The stance during the state of beginnings is receptivity; the stance during the state of struggle is letting go; and the stance of vision culminates in activity. We revisit each stance continually, for they are the aspects of life through which we spiral toward God.

We experience receiving and giving, losing and finding anew, in the ebb and flow of life, but we articulate them separately for the sake of clarity. Clarity, vision, reason, goals, and dreaming are aspects of the North. Its image is the mountaintop or pyramid, the place of vision, and thus the sign of the north is the *triangle*. These images and symbols are embodied in persons and communities who climb their "mountains," like Tabor for Moses and dreaming dreams for Martin Luther King, Jr. The climbs are difficult, steep, and filled with switchbacks that keep travelers from knowing just how far along they have come on their journey. Is it any wonder that hermitages, churches, and monasteries are often built on mountaintops?

Scriptural Reflection

The gospel of the North is *John*, who is symbolized by the eagle. This gospel is ethereal, highlighting the creative breath of life, speech and petition:

> "I will ask the Father
> and he will give you another Advocate
> to be with you always,
> the Spirit of truth."
>
> —John 14:16–17

The prophet of the Hebrew scriptures who accompanies us in the North is *Daniel.* The Book of Daniel, with its dreams and visions and promise of deliverance, finds a home in the heart of the hopeful. Michael, whose name means "How Like Unto God," is the archangel of the North. This angel helps us realize that every single activity, every plan or decision, is permeated with *ruah*, the breath of life, the Spirit of God. *Ruah* is a West-Semitic word.[12] It is an example of onomatopoeia, that is, saying the word makes the sound itself. *Ruah* connotes the strength of life that comes with breathing in and breathing out. It comprises everything that moves persons from within and affects them from the outside. The word *ruah* is used in scripture to explain how God touches human persons and carries them along precisely in God's breathtaking power (Gn 1:2). *Ruah* is bestowed as gift, according to the prophet Isaiah:

> Here is my servant whom I uphold,
> my chosen one, with whom I am pleased,
> Upon whom I have put my spirit;
> he shall bring forth justice to the nations.
>
> —Isaiah 42:1

Ruah is given to the Servant of Yahweh, the Messiah, and it gifts him with the virtues of his ancestors: the wisdom and insight of Solomon and Deborah, the heroism and prudence of David and Esther, and the knowledge and fear of the Lord that characterize Abraham, Jacob, Moses, Sarah, and Ruth. At the end of time the whole people will be given *ruah*. This promise is developed most potently in Ezekiel 37:6 and in Deutero-Isaiah. The people receive *ruah* as a blessing, a holy rain that will make the desert bloom (Is 44:1-5).

As time went by, the term *ruah* became more general. In the psalms *ruah* is seen as the inner life of the person; it shapes the identity of a person's true self.

Application to Forgiving

The Spirit of Yahweh, *ruah*, is the breath that gives life, inspiration, creativity, and the ability to speak the word of God. *Ruah* forms and informs life. Just as when one breathes in the body expands, and when one breathes out the body contracts, so we are called when living in *ruah* to expand our horizons, reach out to others, and, at the same time, contract and center upon God within. Incorporating both elements of *ruah* is necessary for our life and spirit. The depth with which we partake of each will determine the quality and richness of our spiritual lives, much as the depth of our physical breathing affects the health and condition of our bodies. As we live in *ruah*, we become the living breath of God, bringing life, hope, and the promise that God will *be* there for each person in our world. To breathe as one with God has consequences of hope and liberation and power for the world. If we are transformed by that breath and informed by the very life and energy of God it represents, then the power of the Almighty will have a home in us, and we will have the generosity of soul required to forgive those who have seriously wounded us.

The place of maturity is the home of decision-making. Now that we have brought to consciousness the injury and have experienced the damage to our lives, we come to a fork in the road, a moment of choice. We can allow the pain to continue to harm us; we can continue to allow ourselves to be defined by the injury. Or we can dismantle its hold on our lives by choosing to forgive. R. S. Downie stresses that "forgiveness here is an episode which involves the conscious removal of the barrier which injury has raised."[13] It takes faith, generosity, and magnanimity of soul to disengage from the desire for vengeance or the hope that the injurer will change, express regret, or even make the initial effort at reconciliation. Those are the strings that keep us tied to our pain. We are not in the North by accident. Our choice is a response to the call for growth. We accept being here, though we long for the comfort and warmth of not knowing or denying that our lives were anything but whole and peaceful. In this place of maturity, we opt for freedom. The decision to forgive is a choice for quality of life for ourselves and the whole earth. It is, as Hannah Arendt says, "the only reaction which does not merely re-act but acts anew and unexpectedly, unconditioned, by the act that provoked it, therefore freeing from it consequences both the one who forgives and the one who is forgiven."[14]

The North is the place of responsibility, discipline, and the right use of power—for ourselves and for others. Here we choose, with full knowledge, to forgive. We know we are not alone as we embark on a path that may be full of fear and ridicule.

> *As you undertake this journey, breathe deeply, breathe the life of God, using the mantra "I Am With You"; that is, saying the name of God as you breathe. Inhale while saying "I Am," filling your lungs, belly, and whole being with the reality of life and the life of God that is within you. Exhale saying "With You," allowing your breath to fall over you like a waterfall, conscious of the fact that God is within you and greater than you. God is more*

yourself than you, and God continually teaches you to choose to be like Michael, "How Like Unto God." Do this mantra exercise daily for ten or fifteen minutes to allow the power of ruah *to fill your mind, heart, and being, and to give you strength in your commitment to forgive.*

Draw your mandala for today. Contemplate its message to you. Share whatever part of it you choose with a companion or the group.

But to those who did accept him
he gave power to become children of God,
to those who believe in his name, who were born not by natural generation nor by human choice nor by a man's decision but of God.
And the Word *became flesh*
and made his dwelling among us,
and we saw his glory . . .
full of grace and truth.

—John 1:12–14

The Transformation: Seeing Anew

Transformation, Spirit, light, and renewed energy for and within the community are some characteristics of the *East*. Its element is *fire*. The color of the East is *yellow*, and its religious symbols are the *morning star*, *resurrection*, and *rebirth*. We arrive at this new dawn place only after having taken part in this cyclic journey of life. We return, each time at a new level. We spiral toward God. Therefore the *spiral*, the sign of growth, change, evolution, and renewal is most appropriate. This is a place of *creativity*, and its virtue is *wisdom*. The archangel who accompanies us here is *Uriel*, which means "Light of God."

As we come to the East we are transformed. Union with God can be experienced while on earth. The effect of this transformation is an explosion of activity. The fruit of transformation is expansion, with renewed vitality, into the community. In the East we praise and give glory to God, who has accompanied us most intimately along our forgiving journey of awakening, suffering, choosing, and finally becoming free. The most fitting prayer for the East is that of *praise*. Here we say, along with Meister Eckhart, "For all who are active in the light are soaring toward God, free and unencumbered of all that is intermediary. Their light is their works and their works are their light."[15]

The Hebrew prophet who accompanies us in the East is *Ezekiel*, whose preaching of the new heart and the new spirit God creates in the people parallels what happens when we are transformed by forgiving.

> Then he said to me: Prophesy to the spirit, prophesy, son of man, and say to the spirit: Thus says the Lord GOD: From the four winds come, O spirit, and breathe into these slain that they may come to life. I prophesied as he told me, and the spirit came into them; they came alive and stood upright, a vast army. (Ez 37:9-10)

The gospel of the East is *Mark*. The focus of Mark's gospel is the person of Christ, the Messiah, the fulfillment of the promise. Mark is represented by a lion in religious art. This is the image for the male, for the Christ, for feasting, and for the sun. Since the focus of the gospel of Mark is the person of Jesus Christ, the Messiah, it is important to reflect on how Jesus is portrayed as the fulfillment of the promise, as the personalization of God among us.

Scriptural Reflection

Jesus claims to be the Messiah when he tells the Samaritan woman, the disciples, and even Pilate, "I am he," "You've said it." Peter and Martha proclaim Jesus as the Messiah, the Son of God. We can also look at the fruits of the life of Jesus, comparing them to the promised effects of the coming of the Messiah, and see that Jesus is the fulfillment and the perfection of the promise.

The first notable effect of the coming of the Messiah, and one of the fruits of the Spirit, *ruah*, is *joy*. In speaking with the Samaritan woman Jesus promises that

> "whoever drinks the water I shall give will never
> thirst;
> the water I shall give will become in him a spring
> of water
> welling up to eternal life."
>
> —John 4:14

Joy, like this living water, bubbles up from inside us.

The second effect of the coming of the Messiah is *enlightenment*. We see that God is in our midst; thus we see with the eyes of wisdom. This seeing, as light in darkness, becomes the source of our strength, the focus of our hope, and the impetus for our transformation. Jesus says simply, "I am the light of the world" (Jn 9:5).

Jesus is the personification of God, who is gentle and compassionate. Therefore Jesus can say, "I am the good shepherd" (Jn 10:11). Other signs of the Messiah are that *truth* will reign and *paradox* will blossom; for example, we must lose our life to save it (Mt 16:25), and "many who are first will be last; and the last will be first" (Mt 19:30). The truth hidden in paradox helps us see with the eyes of God; we become aware that things are not what they seem.

Application to Forgiving

God calls us home before we actually die. Yahweh made a home with the people; the Messiah was very much at home with his contemporaries, and we also are asked to make our home in and with God. Jesus invited us to "remain in me as I remain in you" (Jn 15:4). The Messiah does not just bring the promise. The Messiah *is* the promise fulfilled. As such, he, the loving presence of God, transforms our lives.

We seem to wallow in fear whenever we do not trust the truth and reality of God as lovingly present. Being in the East moves us out of the grip of the fear of abandonment. Jesus says,

> "Do not let your hearts be troubled.
> You have faith in God;
> and faith also in me."
>
> —John 14:1

The New Testament reveals that attributes of the king–messiah, the son of David, and the servant of Yahweh are united in the person of Jesus. Jesus himself claims to be the Messiah, the Suffering Servant. When preaching in the synagogue of Nazareth, Jesus read aloud from scripture:

> "The Spirit of the Lord is upon me,
> because he has anointed me
> to bring glad tidings to the poor.
> He has sent me to proclaim liberty to captives
> and recovery of sight to the blind,
> to let the oppressed go free,
> and to proclaim a year acceptable to the Lord."
>
> Rolling up the scroll, he handed it back to the attendant and sat down, and the eyes of all in the synagogue looked intently at him. He said to them,

> "Today this scripture passage is fulfilled in your hearing." (Lk 4:18-21)

We know the good news message that we are loved and precious was given long ago, but now it is ours to see, accept, and assimilate at a new level of understanding. Even as we listen, we know the liberation God offers calls for detachment from our pain and our ego's desire for revenge. We are free to accept this spiritual liberation. The voice of God calling us to life anew becomes more than a loud whisper. It becomes a song.[16] Our being in the East is beautifully expressed in an inward and outward spiral dance. In forgiving, we are transformed and freed of the resentment and pain that heretofore had been so oppressive. In the East, even if we must remain in a state of physical oppression, we perceive it with new, free eyes, and we rejoice like Jesus, who prayed to God, "Father, forgive them, for they know not what they do" (Lk 23:34); like the martyrs, who sang as they were being led to their death; and like Etty Hillesum, who rejoiced in the beauty of a rainbow shortly before her death in Auschwitz.

> This morning there was a rainbow over the camp and the sun shone in the mudpuddles. When I entered the sick barrack several women called me over and asked: "Do you have good news? You look so happy."[17]

Titus Brandsma is another example of a person able to live in peace, serenity, and great joy while continually forgiving his oppressors. Brandsma was a Dutch Carmelite, a mystic, a professor at the University of Nijmegen, and a writer who could not be silent in the face of Nazi oppression. Brandsma died in Dachau.

> He lived simply and unobtrusively with a constant, patient smile of inner peace. It was the smile of mystical detachment from all the suffering he had to endure. He was so mistreated that his teeth were literally shook loose in his mouth. Yet, he bore everything with the prayer of Jesus, "Father, forgive them . . . " Never did I nor anyone else ever hear him complain. He was a holy one.[18]

CONCLUSION

We have fine examples, not only in Jesus, the martyrs, and well-known courageous heroes and heroines, but also among ordinary people who are transformed by forgiving and in their forgiving are able to reach out in compassion. The homemaker, the farmer, the teacher, the mother, the survivor, the lost child—every person—is capable of the magnanimity of soul that comes with forgiving and loving unconditionally. They, you, and I, ordinary people, affect the condition of the world beyond imagining by exercising our power to forgive. As Doris Donnelly says, "When forgiveness occurs, an event of cosmic proportions takes place: divisions are healed and the world moves closer to the state in which it was created."[19] We alter the face of the earth by our participation in that "matter of choice" that opens our hearts to that "moment of grace" when forgiving happens.

The Quaternity of the Whole: The Universal Flow

directions	south	west	north	east
characteristics	warmth	darkness	maturity	new life
movements	beginnings	losses	concern for others	joy
images	ocean	desert	mountain	morning star
seasons	summer	autumn	winter	spring
elements	water	earth	air	fire
colors	red	black	white	yellow
virtues	respect	courage	generosity	wisdom
mystical experiences	breakthrough	receptivity	activity	transformation
shapes within the circle	square	cross	triangle	spiral
major prophets	Jeremiah	Isaiah	Daniel	Ezekiel
gospels	Matthew	Luke	John	Mark
prayer forms	thanksgiving	sorrow	petition	praise
scriptural reflections	Elohim	Suffering Servant	Ruah	Jesus, the fulfillment of the promise
forgiveness process	discovering the injury	appoaching compassion	choosing to forgive	seeing anew

Notes

Chapter 1: The Human Need to Forgive

1. Let me stress that forgiveness and reconciliation are separate but related issues. Forgiveness is one essential element for the sacrament of reconciliation along with sin, sorrow, change of heart, and penance. However, reconciliation is not necessarily a consequence of forgiving.

2. Joanna North, "Wrongdoing and Forgiveness," *Philosophy* 62 (1987): 502.

3. Doris Donnelly, *Learning to Forgive* (Nashville: Abingdon Press, 1979), 32.

4. Hannah Arendt, *The Human Condition* (Garden City: Doubleday, 1959), 178-79.

5. Arendt, *The Human Condition*, 214.

6. Virgil Elizondo, "I Forgive But I Do Not Forget," *Concilium* 184 (1986): 74–75.

7. Arendt, *The Human Condition*, 361.

8. Ibid., 213.

9. North, "Wrongdoing and Forgiveness," 508.

10. George Soares-Prabhu, "As We Forgive: Interhuman Forgiveness in the Teaching of Jesus," *Concilium* 184 (1986): 60.

11. Elizondo, "I Forgive But I Do Not Forget," 78.

12. For a list of ten probable consequences of non-forgiving see Donnelly, *Learning to Forgive*, 32.

13. For an explanation of how "guilt may remain a companion on our journey" despite forgiveness, see James D. Whitehead and Evelyn Eaton Whitehead, *Shadows of the Heart: A Spirituality of the Painful Emotions* (New York: Crossroad, 1996), chap. 9.

14. These refinements were presented by Professor Enright at a Parish Staff Reflection Day entitled, "Forgiving Those Who Hurt Us," Madison, Wisconsin, October 20, 1992.

15. North, "Wrongdoing and Forgiveness," 506.

16. Robert Enright, "Must a Christian Require Repentance Before Forgiving?" *Journal of Psychology and Christianity* 9 (1990): 19.

17. Beverly Flanigan, *Forgiving the Unforgivable: Overcoming the Bitter Legacy of Intimate Wounds* (New York: Macmillan, 1992), 17.

18. John H. Hebl and Robert D. Enright, "Forgiveness as a Psychotherapeutic Goal with Elderly Females," paper presented at the University of Wisconsin, Madison (1991), 3.

19. See chapters 5-10 in Sidney B. Simon and Suzanne Simon, *Forgiveness: How to Make Peace with Your Past and Get on with Your Life* (New York: Warner Books, 1990).

20. Joan Borysenko, *Guilt Is the Teacher, Love Is the Lesson* (New York: Warner Books, 1990), 175.

21. John Patton, *Is Human Forgiveness Possible?: A Pastoral Care Perspective* (Nashville: Abingdon Press, 1985), 176.

22. Robert Enright asked this question during an interview on February 11, 1994, at the University of Wisconsin, Madison.

23. Flanigan, *Forgiving the Unforgivable*, 140.

24. Borysenko, *Guilt Is the Teacher, Love Is the Lesson*, 176.

25. Raymond Studzinski, "Remember and Forgive: Psychological Dimensions of Forgiveness," *Concilium* (1986): 17.

26. Joseph Beatty, "Forgiveness," *American Philosophical Quarterly* 7: 3 (1970): 247.

27. Ann Moritfee, in collaboration with David Feinstein, Ph.D., "Healing Journey," *Serenade at the Doorway* (West Vancouver: Mabela Music, 1990).

28. Mary O'Driscoll, O.P., *Catherine of Siena* (Strasbourg: Editions du Signe, 1994), 22.

29. Mary Ann Fatula, O.P., *Catherine of Siena's Way* (Wilmington: Michael Glazier, 1987), 146.

30. Theories of human, moral, and stage development and their universal applications are brought into question by researchers like Heinz Kohut, *The Analysis of the Self: A Systematic Approach to the Psychoanalytic Treatment of Narcissistic Personality Disorders* (New York: International University Press, 1971), 230. For an explanation of how women do not fit the linear pattern for human moral development see Carol Gilligan, *In a Different Voice: Psychological*

Theory and Women's Development (Cambridge: Harvard University Press, 1982). For studies that bring into question stage development itself, claiming that infants take "quantum leaps" in human growth, see Daniel Stern, *The Interpersonal World of the Infant: A View from Psychoanalysis and Developmental Psychology* (New York: Basic Books, 1985), 5.

31. Merle A. Fossum and Marilyn J. Mason, *Facing Shame: Families in Recovery* (New York: W. W. Norton & Company, 1986), 5.

32. Wilkie Au, S.J., and Noreen Cannon, C.S.J., "The Plague of Perfectionism," *Human Development* 13:3 (1992): 9.

33. Kohut, *The Analysis of the Self*, 328.

34. Shaina Noll, words and music by Libby Roderick, "How Could Anyone," *Songs of the Inner Child* (Santa Fe: Singing Heart Productions, 1992).

35. This guided meditation is my adaptation of a format presented by Patricia Burke, Ph.D., during a centering retreat at Sinsinawa, Wisconsin, in 1987. Letting go of various aspects of the human person connects us with our essence.

36. Richard B. Patterson, *Encounters with Angels: Psyche and Spirit in the Counseling Situation* (Chicago: Loyola University Press, 1992), 78.

37. During World War II, Corrie Ten Boom and her sister, Betsie, were sent to the concentration camp at Ravensbruck for helping the Jews in Holland. For their story see Corrie Ten Boom with John and Elizabeth Sherrill, *The Hiding Place* (New York: Bantam Books, 1971), 179–80.

38. Ibid., 236.

39. Lance Morrow, "'I Spoke As a Brother': A Pardon from the Pontiff, A Lesson in Forgiveness for a Troubled World," *Time* (January 19, 1984), 31.

40. Morrow, "I Spoke As a Brother," 28.

41. Translations used in this book are by Martha Alken, O.P., from the original Dutch. *Etty: De Nagelaten Geschriften van Etty Hillesum, 1941–43 [Etty: The Postumous Writings of Etty Hillesum, 1941–43]* (Amsterdam: Balans, 1986), 322. See also an earlier translation of segments of Etty's diaries, *An Interrupted Life* (New York: Pantheon Books, 1983).

42. Ibid., 657.
43. Ibid., 517.
44. Donnelly, *Learning to Forgive*, 66.

Chapter 2: Forgiving and the Question of God

1. Meister Eckhart, "Sermon Fourteen: 'Letting God Be God in You,'" in *Breakthrough: Meister Eckhart's Creation Spirituality in New Translation*, introduction and commentaries by Matthew Fox (New York: Doubleday, 1980), 201.
2. Carol A. Newsom, "Job," *The Women's Bible Commentary*, ed. Carol A. Newsom and Sharon H. Ringe (Louisville: Westminster/John Knox Press, 1992), 132.
3. Donald Capps, *Reframing: A New Method in Pastoral Care* (Minneapolis: Fortress Press, 1990), 145–46.
4. Harold S. Kushner, *When Bad Things Happen to Good People* (New York: Avon Books, 1981), 58.
5. Ibid., 148.
6. C. G. Jung, *Answer to Job*, trans. R. F. C. Hull (London: Ark Paperbacks, 1984), 63.
7. Peter Ellis, "Jeremiah," *The Collegeville Bible Commentary*, Diane Bergant, C.S.A., and Robert J. Karris, O.F.M., general editors (Collegeville: The Liturgical Press, 1989), 453.
8. William L. Holladay, *Jeremiah: Spokesman out of Time* (Philadelphia: Pilgrim Press, 1974), 75.
9. Ibid., 93.
10. Ibid., 103.
11. Kathleen M. O'Connor, "Jeremiah," *The Women's Bible Commentary*, 174.
12. Carroll Stuhlmueller, "Reading Guide: Jeremiah," *The Catholic Study Bible: The New American Bible*, ed. Donald Senior, Mary Ann Getty, Carroll Stuhlmueller, and John J. Collins (New York: Oxford University Press, 1990), 306.
13. Ellis, "Jeremiah," 454.
14. Robert Enright, "Must a Christian Require Repentance Before Forgiving?" *Journal of Psychology and Christianity* 9 (1990):18.
15. Donald Senior, C.P., and Carroll Stuhlmueller, C.P., *The Biblical Foundations for Mission* (Maryknoll, N.Y.: Orbis Books, 1983), 147.

16. Ibid., 148.

17. See Matthew 5:23–25, 6:12, 14–15, 19:18, 26:28; Mark 11:25; Luke 7:48–50, 15:20–24, 17:3–4, 23:24; John 2:1–2, 20:23; 1 John 1:9; Acts 10:43; Ephesians 1:7, 4:31–32; Colossians 3:12–15.

18. Senior and Stuhlmueller, *The Biblical Foundations for Mission*, 263.

19. Doris Donnelly, *Learning to Forgive* (Nashville: Abingdon Press, 1979), 119.

20. Morton T. Kelsey, *God Dreams, and Revelation: A Christian Interpretation of Dreams* (Minneapolis: Augsburg Publishing House, 1974), 23.

21. Walter Brueggemann, *The Prophetic Imagination* (Minneapolis: Fortress Press, 1978), 105.

22. Jacqui Bishop and Mary Grunte, *How to Forgive When You Don't Know How* (New York: Station Hill Press, 1993), 109.

Chapter 3: A Theological Reflection on Forgiving

1. Edward Schillebeeckx, *Jesus: An Experiment in Christology* (New York: Seabury Press, 1978).

2. William Klassen, *The Forgiving Community* (Philadelphia: Westminster Press, 1966), 145–46.

3. See the "Sacrament of Penance Study," *Origins: CNS Documentary Service* 19:38 (1990): 621.

4. Bruce Vawter, C.M., "The Gospel According to John," *The Jerome Biblical Commentary*, ed. Raymond Brown, S.S., Joseph Fitzmer, S.J., Roland E. Murphy, O.Carm. (New York: Prentice-Hall, 1968), 464.

5. Raymond E. Brown, *The Anchor Bible: The Gospel According to John* (New York: Doubleday, 1970), 1042.

6. Ibid., 1041.

7. Christian Duquoc, "The Forgiveness of God," *Concilium* (1986): 34.

8. Ibid.

9. Brown, *The Anchor Bible: The Gospel According to John*, 1044.

10. George A. Aschenbrenner, S.J., S.T.D., "The Inner Journey of Forgiveness," *Human Development* 10:3 (1989): 16.

11. Paul Ricoeur, *The Symbolism of Evil* (New York: Harper & Row, 1967), 233.

12. Edward Farley, *Good and Evil: Interpreting a Human Condition* (Minneapolis: Fortress Press, 1990), 125. Farley's chapter on idolatry is especially worth noting. He explains the classical concept of sin, its problematic features, and the bravado it takes to exist in a world without idols.

13. Loretta Dornisch, *Faith and Philosophy in the Writings of Paul Ricoeur* (New York: The Edwin Mellen Press, 1990), 147.

14. Farley, *Good and Evil*, 127.

15. Karl Menninger, *Whatever Became of Sin?* (New York: Hawthorn Books, 1973), 46.

16. Judith Plaskow, *Sex, Sin and Grace: Women's Experience and the Theologies of Reinhold Niebuhr and Paul Tillich* (New York: University Press of America, 1980), 92.

17. Doris Donnelly, *Seventy Times Seven: Forgiveness and Peace-making* (Erie, Penn.: Benet Press, 1993), ii.

18. Ibid., 16.

19. Hugh Ross Mackintosh, *The Christian Experience of Forgiveness* (London: Collins Clear-Type Press, 1961), 33.

20. Beverly Flanigan, *Forgiving the Unforgivable: Overcoming the Bitter Legacy of Intimate Wounds* (New York: Macmillan, 1992), 220–21.

21. Duquoc, "The Forgiveness of God," 40.

22. Virgil Elizondo, "I Forgive But I Do Not Forget," *Concilium* 184 (1986): 75.

23. Mary Catherine Hilkert, O.P., "Preachers of Transforming Grace," talk given to the Dominican Leadership Conference, Newark, New Jersey (October 1991), 2.

24. Elizabeth Dreyer, "What's So Amazing About Grace?," *U.S. Catholic* 58:5 (May 1993): 9.

25. William A. Barry, S.J., "Breaking the Cycle of Evil," *Human Development* 10:3 (1989): 25.

26. Corrie Ten Boom, *The Hiding Place* (New York: Bantam Books, 1974), 238.

27. Dornisch, *Faith and Philosophy in the Writings of Paul Ricoeur*, 182.

28. Karl Rahner and H. Vorgrimler, "Grace: God's Invitation to Us to Participate in Divine Life," *The Dictionary of Theology* (New York: Crossroad, 1981), 198.

29. Karl, Rahner, "Grace," *Encyclopedia of Theology: The Concise Sacramentum Mundi* (New York: The Seabury Press, 1975), 589.
30. Rahner and Vorgrimler, "Grace: God's Invitation to Us to Participate in Divine Life," 200.
31. Klassen, *The Forgiving Community*, 215.

Chapter 4: Forgiving as a Family Affair

1. Larry Kent Graham, *Care of Persons, Care of Worlds: A Psychosystems Approach to Pastoral Care and Counseling* (Nashville: Abingdon Press, 1992), 77. For an excellent and concise description of family secrets and their effects, see also Edwin H. Friedman, *Generation to Generation: Family Process in Church and Synagogue* (New York: The Guilford Press, 1985), 52–54.
2. For a readable and inspiring treatment of grief, loss, pain and healing, see Alla Bozarth-Campbell, *Life Is Goodbye, Life Is Hello: Grieving Well Through All Kinds of Loss* (Minneapolis: CompCare Publications, 1985), 49.
3. For a clear, concise explanation of forgiveness see Joanna North, "Wrongdoing and Forgiveness," *Philosophy* 62 (1987): 499–508.
4. William J. Worden, *Grief Counseling and Grief Therapy: A Handbook for the Mental Health Practitioner* (New York: Springer Publishing Company, 1991), 118.
5. Evelyn and James Whitehead, *Seasons of Strength: New Visions of Adult Christian Maturing* (New York: Doubleday, 1984), 126.
6. Augustus Y. Napier, with Carl Whitaker, *The Family Crucible: The Intense Experience of Family Therapy* (New York: Harper Perennial, 1978), 80.
7. For a comprehensive overview of the literature on family, as system, see Dorothy Stroh Becvar and Raphael J. Becvar, *Family Therapy: A Systemic Integration* (Boston: Allyn and Bacon, 1993), 156.
8. Brian J. Kelly, "A Theory About Families Can Benefit Communities," *Human Development* 15:2 (1994): 23–27.
9. Ernest Kurtz and Katherine Ketcham, *The Spirituality of Imperfection: Modern Wisdom from Classic Stories* (New York: Bantam Books, 1992), 214.

10. Joan Borysenko, *Guilt Is the Teacher, Love Is the Lesson: A Book to Heal You, Heart and Soul* (New York: Warner Books, 1990), 211.

Chapter 5: Forgiving Systemic Injury

1. R. S. Downie, "Forgiveness," *The Philosophical Quarterly* 15 (1965), 128–34. This article is foundational for much of the recent literature on forgiveness.

2. Kat Duff, *The Alchemy of Illness* (New York: Bell Tower, 1993), 121.

3. Downie,"Forgiveness," 131.

4. John H. Hebl and Robert D. Enright, "Forgiveness as a Psychotherapeutic Goal with Elderly Females" [a paper] (Madison: University of Wisconsin, 1991): 1.

5. Donald Senior, C.P., and Carroll Stuhlmueller, C.P., *The Biblical Foundations of Mission* (Maryknoll, N.Y.: Orbis Books, 1993), 263.

6. Doris Donnelly, *Learning to Forgive* (Nashville: Abingdon Press, 1979), 119.

7. Senior and Stuhlmueller, *The Biblical Foundations of Mission*, 151.

8. Larry Kent Graham, *Care of Persons, Care of Worlds: A Psychosystems Approach to Pastoral Care and Counseling* (Nashville: Abingdon Press, 1992), 39.

9. Edwin H. Friedman, *Generation to Generation: Family Process in Church and Synagogue* (New York: The Guilford Press, 1985), 15.

10. Ludwig von Bertalanffy, *General System Theory: Foundations, Development, Applications* (New York: George Braziller, 1968), 39.

11. Ibid., 70.

12. Ibid., 159.

13. For an excellent articulation of pastoral care needs of women, by women, see Maxine Glaz and Jeanne Stevenson Moessner, eds. *Women in Travail and Transition: A New Pastoral Care* (Minneapolis: Fortress Press, 1991), 51.

14. Von Bertalanffy, *General System Theory*, 207.

15. Carl Reinhold Bråkenhielm, *Forgiveness* (Minneapolis: Fortress Press, 1993), 34.

16. John Patton, *Is Human Forgiveness Possible?: A Pastoral Care Perspective* (Nashville: Abingdon Press, 1985), 176.

17. Interview with Nathan Elbaum, August 1, 1995. Nathan lives in Madison, Wisconsin, and gives presentations to students about his experiences as a survivor of the concentration camps of World War II.

18. Patricia Wittberg, S.C., "Outward Orientation in Declining Organizations: Reflections on the LCWR Documents," in *Claiming Our Truth: Reflections on Identity by United States Women Religious*, ed. Nadine Foley, O.P. (Washington D. C.: Leadership Conference of Women Religious, 1988), 99. For an excellent historical overview of how communities of women religious have adapted and flourished in spite of oppressive systems of church and society, see Mary Ewens, O.P., *The Role of the Nun in Nineteenth Century America* (Salem: Ayer Company, 1971).

19. Ibid., 92.

20. For an excellent summary of the development of religious life as a system and a hopeful perspective on its future, see Diarmuid O'Murchu, *Religious Life: A Prophetic Vision* (Notre Dame, Ind.: Ave Maria Press, 1991), 37.

21. Carol Osiek, R.S.C.J., *Beyond Anger: On Being a Feminist in the Church* (New York: Paulist Press, 1986), 46. Quoted from Elisabeth Schüssler Fiorenza, "Sexism and Conversion," *Network* 9:3 (1981): 15–22.

22. Ibid., 50-51.

23. Evelyn and James Whitehead, *Seasons of Strength: New Visions of Adult Christian Maturing* (New York: Doubleday, 1984), 126–27.

Chapter 6: The Fourfold Journey of Forgiving

1. Angeles Arrien, as a cultural anthropologist, has studied the meanings of symbols and myths from a cross-cultural perspective. Arrien presents the significance of the five universal signs and how to use them as tools to greater self-knowledge and deeper understanding of others with whom we live and work. See Angeles Arrien, *Signs of Life: The Five Universal Shapes and How to Use Them* (Sonoma: Argus Publishing Company, 1992).

2. *The Sacred Pipe: Black Elk's Account of the Seven Rites of the Oglala Sioux*, ed. Joseph Brown (New York: Penguin Books, 1971). See page 5 for an excellent overview of the symbols for the four directions.

3. C. G. Jung, *Mandala Symbolism*, trans. R. F. C. Hull (Princeton: Prinston University Press, 1972), 5.

4. Ibid., 40–41.

5. For a more complete description of a mandala of angels, see Joan Borysenko, *Pocketful of Miracles: Prayers, Meditations, and Affirmations to Nurture Your Spirit Every Day of the Year* (New York: Warner Books, 1994), 5–9.

6. The concepts surrounding Elohim were taken from the class "Bijbelse Spiritualiteit" ["Biblical Spirituality"], given by Dr. Kees Waaijman, during the fall semester, 1985, at the University of Nijmegen. The notes were translated by Martha Alken, O.P.

7. Beverly Flanigan presents a six-stage process for forgiveness based on reason and aimed at self-renewal. See Beverly Flanigan, *Forgiving the Unforgivable: Overcoming the Bitter Legacy of Intimate Wounds* (New York: Macmillan, 1992), 71.

8. Ibid., 90.

9. *Breakthrough: Meister Eckhart's Creation Spirituality in New Translation*, introduction and commentaries by Matthew Fox (New York: Doubleday, 1980), 183. Quoted from James Clark and John V. Skinner, *Meister Eckhart: Selected Treatises and Sermons Translated from Latin and German with an Introduction and Notes* (London: Faber & Faber, 1958), 103.

10. *Breakthrough*, 381.

11. Carl Reinhold Bråkenhielm, *Forgiveness*, trans. Thor Hall (Minneapolis: Fortress Press, 1993), 89.

12. The scriptural explanations of the word *ruah* are translated and adapted by this author from Kees Waaijman's introduction to the text by Otger Steggink and Kees Waaijman, *Spiritualiteit en Mystiek [Spirituality and Mysticism]* (Nijmegen: B.V. v/h B. Gottmer's uitgeversbedrijf, 1985), 9–12.

13. See the excellent article on forgiveness by R. S. Downie, "Forgiveness," *The Philosophical Quarterly* 15 (1965): 133.

14. Hannah Arendt, *The Human Condition* (Chicago: University of Chicago Press, 1958), 241.

15. *Breakthrough*, 481.

16. Suggested music for the journey:

South:

Michael Joncas, "My Soul Is Thirsting," *Winter Name of God* (Chicago: CIA Publications, 1988), and Shaina Noll, "How Could Anyone?" *Songs for the Inner Child* (Santa Fe: Singing Heart Productions, 1992).

West:

Ann Morifee in collaboration with David Feinstein, "Healing Journey" and "Anger Is a Fever," *Serenade at the Doorway* (Canada: Mabela Music, 1990).

North:

Gothic Voices, "A Feather on the Breath of God," *Music of Hildegard von Bingen* (New York: Angel Records, 1993).

East:

Massenet, "Meditation from Thaïs," *Boléro and Other French Favorites* (New York: BMG Music, 1990).

As a conclusion for all directions:

David Haas, "Prayer for Peace," *Gather* (Chicago: GIA Publications, 1987), a song based on a Navaho Indian prayer.

17. Etty Hillesum, *Etty: De Nagelaten Geschriften Van Etty Hillesum, 1941–1943* [*Etty: The Postumous Writings of Etty Hillesum, 1941–1943*] (Amsterdam: Balans), 673. Translation mine.

18. Constant Dölle, *Titus Brandsma-Karmeliet* (Amstelveen: Boekmakerij/uitgeverij Luyten-in samenwerking met de Orde van de Nederlandse Karmelieten, 1985), 67. Translation mine.

19. Doris Donnelly, *Learning to Forgive* (Nashville: Abingdon Press, 1979), 99.

For Further Reading

In addition to the books, articles, and tapes cited in the notes, the reader may want to consult the following materials.

Books

Anderson, Terry. *Den of Lions: A Startling Memoir of Survival and Triumph.* New York: Ballatine Books, 1993.

Casarjian, Robin. *Forgiveness: A Bold Choice for a Peaceful Heart.* New York: Bantam Books, 1992.

__________ . *Houses of Healing: A Prisoner's Guide to Inner Power and Freedom.* Boston: Lionheart Press, 1995.

Chittister, Joan, O.S.B. *Job's Daughters: Women and Power.* New York: Paulist Press, 1990.

Dreyer, Elizabeth. *Manifestations of Grace.* Wilmington, Del.: Michael Glazier, 1990.

Golomb, Elan, Ph.D. *Trapped in the Mirror: Adult Children of Narcissists in Their Struggle for Self.* New York: Quill William Morrow, 1992.

Harris, Maria. *Proclaim Jubilee!: A Spirituality for the Twenty-First Century.* Louisville: Westminster/John Knox Press, 1996.

The Herder Dictionary of Symbols: Symbols from Art, Archaelogy, Mythology, Literature, and Religion. Edited by Deborah Farrell and Carole Presser. Translated by Boris Matthews. Wilmette: Chiron, 1993.

Randall, Robert L., Ph.D. *Pastor and Parish: The Psychological Core of Ecclesiastical Conflicts.* New York: Human Sciences Press, 1988.

Schneiders, Sandra M. *Beyond Patching: Faith and Feminism in the Catholic Church.* New York: Paulist Press, 1991.

Smedes, Lewis B. *The Art of Forgiving: When You Need to Forgive and Don't Know How.* Nashville: Moorings, 1996.

Switzer, David K. *The Minister as Crisis Counselor*. Nashville: Abingdon Press, 1990.

Viorst, Judith. *Necessary Losses: The Loves, Illusions, Dependencies, and Impossible Expectations That All of Us Have to Give Up in Order to Grow*. New York: Fawcett Gold Medal, 1986.

Articles

Duquoc, Christian. "Real Reconciliation and Sacramental Reconciliation." In *Sacramental Reconciliation*. Edited by Edward Schillebeeckx. New York: Herder and Herder, 1971.

Enright, Robert. "Five Points on the Construct of Forgiveness Within Psychotherapy," *Psychotherapy* 28 (1991).

Frohlich, M. "Toward a Theology of Religious Life, North American Women, and the Intellectual Life," paper prepared for the Brookland Commission Conference (1992).

Harrison, B. "The Power of Anger in the Work of Love." In *Weaving the Visions: New Patterns in Feminist Spirituality*. Edited by J. Plaskow and C. Christ. San Francisco: Harper & Row, 1989.

Hope, Donald. "The Healing Paradox of Forgiveness," *Psychotherapy* 24 (1987).

Kenel, Mary Elizabeth. "Aging Parents and Our Aging Selves," *Human Development* 16 (1995).

Lang, Berel. "The Holocaust and Two Views of Forgiveness," *Tikkun* 11:2 (1996).

Linn, Matthew, Dennis Linn, and Sheila Fabricant. "Healing Yourself Through Healing the Family Tree," *Praying* 15 (1985).

Malone, Janet, C.N.D. "Exploring Human Anger," *Human Development* 15:1 (1994).

__________. "Forgive But Don't Forget," *Human Development* 15:2 (1994).

Sweetser, T. "Viewing the Parish as a System," *Human Development* 15:2 (1994).

Thompson, Marjorie J. "Moving Toward Forgiveness," *Weavings: A Journal of the Christian Spiritual Life* (12 April 1992).

Tapes

Borysenko, Joan. "*Seventy Times Seven: On the Spiritual Art of Forgiveness*," Sounds True Audio, Boulder, Col., 1996.